Okinawa, Japan

The People, History, World War II, Culture and Tradition. Travel and Tourism

Author

Benjamin Hudson

Copyright Notice

Copyright © 2017 Global Print Digital
All Rights Reserved

First Printing: 2017.

ISBN: 978-1-912483-11-2

Publisher: Global Print Digital.
Arlington Row, Bibury, Cirencester GL7 5ND
Gloucester
United Kingdom.
Website: www.homeworkoffer.com

Table of Content

Introduction

This book covers all parts of Okinawa People's life, including History, Environment, People, Tradition, Diet, and much more. Service interest: Self-Education, Travel and Tourism, Business purposes.

Okinawa was once an independent country which was ruled by the Ryukyu Kingdom, and flourished through trade with China - the largest country in Asia - as well as other neighboring countries. After the invasion of Satsuma in 1609, Ryukyu became a part of Japan's shogunate system. It became a prefecture of Japan due to the Abolition of the Han System and Establishment of the Prefecture System, which occurred in 1879.

During the Pacific War, Okinawa was the site of the only land battle in Japan that involved civilians. After the war, Okinawa was placed under the administration of the United States. In 1972, however, Okinawa was returned to Japanese administration. Okinawa remains under Japanese administration today.

Okinawa Prefecture is the only region in Japan that is in the subtropical zone, and is blessed with a warm climate all year round. An ocean with coral reefs, where schools of colorful tropical fish swim about, sustains various forms of life.

In addition, creatures that are treasured worldwide, such as the Okinawa rail and the Iriomote cat, make their habitats in the forests of the northern part of Okinawa island and Iriomote island.

In December 2000, nine sites - including Shuri Castle Ruins and Nakagusuku Castle Ruins - were registered as world heritage sites and were named "Gusuku Sites and Related Properties of the Kingdom of Ryukyu." It is said that there are nearly 300 gusukus (castles) in the Ryukyu Islands, many of which were constructed on slopes with scenic views. The gusukus that were registered as world heritage sites are believed to have been the residential castles of regional rulers who played an active role during the process of establishment of the Ryukyu Kingdom.

During the Ryukyu Dynasty, the royal government put a great deal of effort into developing performing arts, and royal performing arts such as kumiodori (a traditional narrative dance), buyo (a traditional dance), and music blossomed. Performing arts that were performed in festivals as well as those that were performed for amusement purposes by commoners also flourished, and are continued to this day. In recent years, the success of musicians and artists from Okinawa has received much attention.

In addition, Okinawa has a variety of traditional crafts including dyed textiles (such as bingata and bashofu), lacquerware, and earthenware, many of which were developed during the Ryukyu Dynasty through cultural exchanges with countries such as China and Japan. Okinawa has developed a distinct aesthetic beauty while being influenced by such cultural exchanges.

Okinawa has a variety of festivals for each season. The festivals range in variety and include: festivals for welcoming the spirits of ancestors, festivals for wishing a good harvest and abundant fish catches, and festivals for keeping away plagues. The regional flavors are also rich.

While we cherish traditional festivals, new festivals that incorporate Okinawan history, culture, and traditional performing arts, such as the All-Okinawa Eisa Festival and the Ryukyu Kingdom Royal Procession, have also been created.

Okinawa is one of the world's leaders in longevity. Some of the factors that have sustained this longevity include: a warm climate, the easygoing personalities of the locals, the spirit of "yumaru" (helping one another), and the traditional food culture.As for the food culture in particular, the idea of "healthy diet, healthy body" has become widely accepted in Okinawa, influenced by cultural exchanges with China.

Okinawan cooking includes royal cuisine, which was developed to serve the Chinese emperor's envoys or officials from Satsuma, and commoners' dishes which were developed to suit the lives of common people.

History

Prehistory of Okinawa

Okinawa lies at the southwest tip of the Japanese archipelago and consists of a chain of a great number of islands. Presently the islands of Okinawa are sandwiched between the Japanese mainland and continental Asia but in ancient times they were connected to the Asian continent. There was migration from the continent by flora and fauna as evidenced by fossils unearthed in excavations.

It is not clear when humans came to inhabit the islands but fossil human bones from the Yamashita-cho Cave 1, excavated in Naha City, have been positively dated to 32,000 years ago and, in Gushigami-son village, the remains of the Minatogawa people have been dated to 17,000 years ago. These Paleolithic humans are thought to have crossed over on a land bridge from continental China but exact details remain unknown.

From the era of the Minatogawa humans there is a blank spot in our knowledge for about 10,000 years until the Neolithic era, around 7,000 years ago. This period in Japan extends through the Jomon Period (to 200BC) and is divided into the Early, First-half, Middle, Late, and Final Jomon Periods and as well as the Yayoi Period (200BC to 250AD). The Early and First-half of the Jomon period was one of thriving exchange between Okinawa and Kyushu. The middle period saw the development of independent cultures on the Okinawa and Amami Islands but the exchanges with Kyushu resumed in the Late Jomon. By the end of the Jomon, villages were forming and there appears to have been contact with China as well. These periods can be said to have been eras of active exchange with Kyushu.

In the Yayoi there are many remains in the coastal sand dunes where artifacts show trade with both Kyushu and China. Shells of Tricornis latissimus shellfish, used as raw material for making shell products, are typical of goods transported to Kyushu at that time. Aside from the earthenware brought in from Kyushu, the custom of burial in box-shaped stone coffins was transferred from Kyushu.

From the Kofun (Tumulus) era (250-552AD) through to the Heian Period (749-1185 AD), the society on the Okinawa and Amami Islands was in the hunter-gatherer stage and there was little contact with mainland Japan.

The Sakishima area, consisting of the Miyako and Yaeyama island groups, formed a different cultural sphere than the Okinawa and Amami island groups. There was no influence from the Jomon and Yayoi cultures and it is thought from existent remains that the Sakishima area had more in common with the southern regions of Asia.

The Paleolithic Age in Okinawa

The Origin of the Ryukyu Island Chain

To the east of continental China, the Ryukyu chain stretches out in the 1,200km between Kyushu and Taiwan. Around the middle of these southern islands is Okinawa Prefecture. The prefecture is composed of 146 islands looking across the vast East China Sea to the continent of China.

From approximately 250 million years ago to 130 million years ago the Ryukyu archipelago was still on the bottom of the ocean. About 15 to 10 million years ago it was connected to Kyushu and continental China. At that time elephants, wild cats and deer migrated across. There have been numerous discoveries such as the so-called living fossil, the Iriomote Island Yamaneko (a wild cat, Mayailurus. Iriomotensis Imaizumi) as well as fossil remains of animals that inhabited the continents of Asia and Japan.

From 10 to 2 million years ago the Ryukyus again separated from other land masses and about 1.5 million years ago, it was connected to continental China. But by 20,000 years ago it had separated completely and broke up into three island groups. By the end of the glacial period the sea level rose 100 meters and the islands became as we see them today

Paleolithic Humans and Culture of the Ryukyu Archipelago

It has been said that humans emerged on earth about 40 million years ago. In Japan, at the Iwajuku site in Gunma Prefecture, flaked stone tools dated about 30,000 years ago have been excavated. In all there are about 5,000 sites in Japan from the Paleolithic age.

While tools have been found in abundance from the Paleolithic era, human remains have not been excavated in any great quantity and there is very little concrete knowledge about the Stone Age humans.

The total picture of Paleolithic humans was made substantially clearer with the discovery of the Minatogawa remains found in 1967 in

Okinawa. It was a complete fossil find showing the skull, hands, and feet of a modern human and was dated to 17.000 years ago. This discovery allowed researchers to get a clear and concrete idea of the appearance of Paleolithic humans and contributed to a great advance in research on the Stone Age.

There have been finds of human fossils in other parts of Okinawa as well; the Yamashita Dojin human in Naha City, the Shimoji-genjin human on Kume-jima Island, and the Pinza-abu human on Miyakojima Island

The Yamashita Dojin and Minatogawa Humans

In 1962 on a Ryukyu limestone plateau on the south side of the Onoyama area of Yamashita-cho, Naha City, in the Yamashita Daiich cave fossilized human remains were discovered. The human fossils excavated here were called the Yamashita Dojin and are believed to be the remains of an 8-year-old girl from 32,000 years ago.

In 1967, in a stone quarry of Gushikami-son, the fossilized remains of 7 Stone Age humans and the fossilized bones of deer and boar were discovered.

The fossils were named after the area where they were found, Minatogawa, and are estimated to be 17.000 years old. The discovery of complete Paleolithic human skeletons with complete skulls, feet and hands were the first such finds in Asia and were of worldwide interest.

The human fossils found at Minatogawa are similar to those of the Peking man (sinanthropus) and the Luijiang human found in continental China. They are said to be the ancestors of the Okinawans living today, but there is much about the Minatogawa humans that remain a mystery. Also there have been very few stone age tools unearthed from Minatogawa sites and details on the lifestyle of these early humans is not known at all.

Fossil Humans and Paleolithic Culture

Within Japan, in the islands of Okinawa, are sites where many human fossils have been discovered.. This is due to the presence of large quantities of calcium carbonate, which leaches out in the substrate water in the Ryukyuan limestone caves of Okinawa. The concentration of calcium carbonate in these stalactite caves has fossilized the bones of humans that were within.

In the digs from other areas of Japan, such as sites in the Kanto region's loam, the acidic nature of the volcanic soil was not conducive to fossilization and most bones dissolved away quickly.

Surveys confirm that there are as many as 600 caves in Okinawa, but most have not been investigated and have been filled in or destroyed. It is desirable to conduct careful study in them because of the possibility of archeological finds within. It is thought that through the advances brought about by investigation and excavation of these stalactite caves, the chances are certain that an increasing number of human fossils will be found.

Name	Estimated Dates	Part of Skeleton Discovered	Year Discovered / Location
Yamashita Dojin	32,0000 years ago	Thighbone of an infant, shinbones, etc.	1962 Naha City
Yonebaru-jin	30,000 years ago (?)	Pelvis, thighbones, clavicle, etc.	1966 Ishigaki City (Ishigaki-shima Island)
Oyama-jin	18,000 years ago	Lower jawbone 1966	Ginowan City
Minatogawa-jin	17,000 years ago	Almost complete skeletons of 4-7 individuals	1967 Gushikami-son
Pinza-abu-jin	26,000 years ago	Parietal and occipital bones	1979 Ueno-son(Miayko-jima Island)
Iegohezu-jin	20,000 years ago	Jawbone, pieces of skull	1977 Ie-son (Iejima Island)
Shimoji-Gendojin	15.000 years ago	Thigh bones of an infant, about 50 pieces of lower jawbone	1983 Gushikawa-son (Kume-jima Island)

The Neolithic Age in Okinawa

The Neolithic Age Cultural Spheres

In the Nanto Islands of the Ryukyu Archipelago there were three prehistoric cultural spheres.

The northern zone comprised Tanegeshima and Yakushima island, of the Satsunan group of islands. The Amami and Ryukyu Island groups comprised the central cultural zone, and the southern zone consisted of the Miyako and Yaeyama island groups.

The Jomon culture of the northern zone moved south into the central zone's Amami and Ryukyu Island groups in the first part of the Jomon period. In those areas there was an independent culture that had already developed and its origin, according to recent archeological excavations, has been found to date from several thousands of years earlier than had previously been thought.

On the other hand, the so-called Sakishima cultural sphere (the Sakishima, Miyako-jima and the Yaeyama Island groups) had a different type of culture than the Jomon and Yayoi cultures of mainland Japan. There were few relations with the Japanese mainland, or the Amami and Okinawa Islands. The Sakishima Islands' roots are deeply related to Taiwan, the Philippines and the southern regions of Asia.

Aspects of Jomon Period Okinawa (1)

Early Jomon(Approx. 10,000 - 8,000 years ago)

Remains from this period consist of the Toguchi Agaribaru ruins of Yomitan-son, the Point B Noguni Shell Mound of Kadena-cho, and the Yabuchi Cave Ruins of Yonashiro-cho. Most of the ruins are situated by the seashore, which indicates a fishing lifestyle for those that lived there. The oldest earthenware pottery in Okinawa is the Tsumegatamon-doki, which have impressions of the makers' fingertips and fingernails on them. This type of pottery is estimated to be around 6,700 years old and is also known as Yabuchi type and Agaribaru type earthenware.

The First-half of the Jomon Period(Approx. 8,000 - 5,000 years ago)
The sites from this period have yielded earthenware produced by Kyushu Jomon peoples and it is thought that boats crossed over from Kyushu bringing these items.

Middle Jomon Period(Approx. 5,000 - 4,000 years ago)
During this period the peoples of the mountainous regions held power in Kyushu and due to this and the enormous amount of volcanic

activity, no Kyushu Jomon culture passed to Okinawa in this period. As a result the prehistoric Nanto central cultural sphere developed its own original culture during this period. Shell mounds have been discovered from this period so it is thought that these people lived in settlements.

Aspects of Jomon Period Okinawa (2)

The Late Jomon Period (Approx. 4000 - 3,000 years ago)

During this period the prehistoric Nanto central cultural sphere developed an independent culture. The biggest influence was the development of the Iha-shiki type and the Ogido-shiki type from the Ichiki-shiki type Kyushu earthenware vessels that had previously been produced. Because of the excavation of dragon and butterfly shaped shell work, it is believed that there were ties with the Chinese continent during this period.

Final Jomon Period (Approx. 3000 - 2,300 years ago)

This period saw the establishment of villages and an increase in the population on the islands. Rudimentary farming was started and excavations have uncovered vessels used for storage. Exchanges with Kyushu occurred frequently and this is believed to have exerted an enormous influence.

Aspects of Yayoi Period Okinawa

Early, Middle, and Late Yayoi Period(Approx. 2,300 - 1,700 years ago)

In this period people who had been living inland on the Ryukyuan limestone hills migrated to the seashore. Excavation of the shell mounds revealed the presence of a large number of giant clam shells used as sinkers leading researchers to believe the people used nets to harvest fish.

The replacement of stone tools for iron and copper utensils from excavations indicate that there was active trading overseas during this period. The Tricornis latissimus and Conidae shells harvested in Amami and Okinawa were transported to Kyushu where they were processed into shell products such as the Kaiwa shell bracelets which were traded throughout the whole of Japan. The products traded for are believed to be Yayoi pottery vessels. The Yayoi period ruins in the prefecture yielded the same type of pottery excavated from Kyushu Yayoi period sites.

The Neolithic Age in Sakishima

Aspects of Neolithic Period Sakishima

In the ruins from prehistoric sites on the islands on the southernmost tip of the Ryukyu archipelago, (the Sakishima. Miyako-jima and Yaeyama Island Groups), there is no apparent influence from Jomon or

Yayoi culture. These islands are believed to have received Philippine and Indonesian influences instead. Perhaps the seas lying between Okinawa and Miyako are the boundary of the Japanese culture's southern expansion.

Contemporary with the Jomon Period (Japan)

Earthenware vessels and stone tools have been found from archeological digs in this period. Pottery of the type designated Shimodabaru, as well as thick reddish brown earthenware without decoration are most typical of vessels from this period. The blades of the stone tools were the only portions of the tools that were polished, unlike those discovered in Okinawa and Amami, so it is thought the primary roots of this culture are from Southeast Asia.

Contemporary with the Yayoi to the Heian Periods (Japan)

Many of the sites from this period can be found near the seashore in sandy areas. The large scale of the culture of this time is its characteristic. Centering on the Yaeyama Islands it extended to the Miyako Islands.

Stone and shell axes have been excavated but the absence of pottery indicates a break with the pottery culture during this period. The use of unsuitable giant clam shells for making axes, examples of which have not been found in Amami and Okinawa, is thought to have been brought over from Southeast Asia and other islands from the south. This period extends from 2,500 BC to the10th century AD.

The Shell Road

The Nansei Island Group including Okinawa and Amami are formed of beautiful coral reefs. The abundant sea life of the area facilitated the use of shells for making products such as knives, axes, and necklaces. The shells and shell work produced in Okinawa was transported north along the warm Kuroshio current and even reached the mainland of Japan some 2,000 years ago during the Yayoi Period. This has been called "The Shell Road" and is a trading route from the Nansei Island Group northward to the north of Kyushu, past the inland Seto Sea across to the Kinki region of the Japanese mainland. The other route on this Shell Road was up the seacoast of Japan via the Genkainada area off the coast of Kyushu.

Recent excavations in Hokkaido, the northernmost island in Japan, have uncovered shell decoration made in the South Seas, a distance of over 2,000 kilometers. The raw materials, mostly Tricornis latissimus and Conidae shells, were transported to the northern part of Kyushu and shaped into shell products and shipped out all across Japan.

That such a magnificent trading operation was being conducted in the

Yayoi is credit to the stable economy of the era and potential for a division of labor that backed it up.

Trading was active along the "The Shell Road" for over 800 years from the Yayoi period (200BC - 250AD) through to the Kofun or Tumulus Period (250 - 552AD). In the Kofun Period the trade brought an increasing variety of shell to the mainland of Japan and the people of Okinawa received grain, products made from metals, and cloth.

Modern Okinawa

The beginning of the 19th century saw the western nations expand nation by nation into Asia. The national seclusion policy was abandoned in Japan and a modern state was established. As part of that process, the Ryukyu Kingdom was incorporated into Japan and the monarchy that had ruled the islands for 500 years was dissolved.

What the future held for the newly established Okinawa Prefecture was down a tumultuous road. Perhaps because of the difference in systems and customs there was a deeply rooted resentment of the old ruling class and the Meiji government in Tokyo. Because of this the Meiji Government adopted the "Ancient Customs Preservation Policy" toward the Ryukyus for the time being.

According to this policy, the landholding system, taxation system, and local government system were all to remain as they were with no great or sudden reforms. This was to avoid any resistance that might come from the Okinawan side. However, the effect of the various policies toward Okinawa resulted in the prefecture falling behind in modernization in comparison to other prefectures and caused the citizens of Okinawa hardships.

The move toward standardizing education to the mainland Japanese standards, along the lines of the Imperial Rescript on Education, began to be thoroughly carried out in the latter half of the 19th century, after the Sino-Japanese War. Subsequent to this, the inexperienced Okinawans were forced into battle in the Russo-Japanese War as members of the Japanese army.

The economic climate in this period of time was that of serious recession. In Okinawa as well, from the latter part of the Taisho Era (1912-1926) to the beginning of the Showa Era (1926-1988) there was widespread economic panic. In this time Okinawans suffered what has been termed the "Cycad Hell", from a type of poisonous palm the people were forced to process and eat to avoid starvation. Many Okinawans opted instead for emigration to mainland Japan and overseas to foreign countries.

As the Showa Era opened, Japanese plans for imperialistic expansion into Asia widened and Okinawa was positioned as the advance base for the defense of the mainland. In March of 1945 it was on the Kerama Island group in Okinawa Prefecture that US Military forces landed and Okinawa entered into the tragic days of the Battle of Okinawa. The Battle of Okinawa resulted in the sacrifice of many people and it can be said to be symbolic of modern Okinawan history shared with mainland Japan.

The Disposition of the Ryukyus

The American Advance in the East

In the start of the 19th century the United States began to consider Japan as a desirable port of call for ships operating in the North Pacific and trading ships going to and from China. In 1846 the US dispatched Commodore Biddle to present demands for opening of Japan but he was turned away by the Tokugawa Shogunate.

The subsequent group dispatched by the US for negotiations with Japan stopped in the Ryukyus before heading to Japan. This time Commodore Perry headed the delegation. The Americans, knowing that the Ryukyu Kingdom was under the control of the Japanese, were thinking of occupying the Ryukyus, should negotiations fail with the Japanese on the mainland. In May 1853 Perry' fleet appeared in the

Ryukyus seeking a treaty of commerce with the Ryukyu Kingdom. While these demands were refused, Perry did succeed in overcoming resistance to a visit to the royal court and he was able to gain admittance to Shurijo Castle.

In June the arrival of Perry's fleet in Uraga on the Japanese mainland resounded throughout Japan. Perry strongly demanded the opening of the country from seclusion and was refused but returned again the following year in March and was able to conclude the Treaty of Kanagawa by a show of strength. In this way the long national seclusion policies of Japan came to an end.

In June of 1854 Commodore Perry again visited the islands and forced the royal court to agree to the "Treaty of Peace and Amity between the Kingdom of the Ryukyus and the United States." The treaty contained provisions prescribing hospitality toward Americans, provisioning of fuel supplies and water, rescue and protection for shipwrecked American sailors, maintenance of the American cemetery, and piloting services.

The Tokugawa Shogunate collapsed under the pressure to open the country from the American and European countries and the modernization of Japan was begun. At the same time this new age became a surging wave in the Ryukyus.

Landfall of American and European Ships on the Ryukyus

1797   British survey ship HMS Providence (Captain William Robert Broughton), Shipwrecked off the coast of the Miyako- Tarama Islands. In the same year the ship headed into Naha Harbor. "A Voyage of Discovery to the North Pacific Ocean" by William Robert Broughton, 1804

1803   British ship HMS Frederick made landfall at Naha Harbor.

1816   British ships Lyra and Alceste arrive in the Ryukyus and stay 42 days. "Account of a Voyage of Discovery to the West Coast of Corea, and the Great Loo-choo Island" London, 1818

1827   British ship HMS Blossom (Captain Frederick Beechey) arrived in the Ryukyus. "Narrative of a Voyage to the Pacific and Beering's Strait" Published 1831

1832   British ship HMS Rodomasuto drifts ashore in the Ryukyus.

1843   British Navy Vessel HMS Samarang makes a land survey of Miyako and Yaeyama Islands. "Narrative Voyage of the HMS Samarang, Published in 1848

1844   French Navy ship Alcmene sails into Naha Harbor seeking friendly relations and trade. Entrusting that a reply to request for trade will be issued to the following ship to call in the Ryukyus, the ship sails on to China leaving behind the missionary Theodore Augustine Focade.

1846   British ship HMS Starling made landfall at Naha Harbor. The English missionary Barnard Bettelheim arrives in the Ryukyus for an 8-year stay. French ship Sabine lands in Naha with Pierre-Julien Le Turdu, successor to Focade. Later the French ships Cleopatoru and Victorious arrive at Unten Harbor seeking reply to the request made in 1844 for friendship and trade relations. They were refused by the Ryukyuans. Visit to Naha of three British fleet vessels. Consent was granted for the start of trade between the Satsuma Han and France.

1847   Ships from western nations visit the Kume-jima, Miyako, Yaeyama and Yonaguni Islands.

1849   British ships arrive requesting commercial relations. . Ships from foreign counties arrive in the Kume-jima and Miyako Islands.

1850   British ship HMS Renard arrives. .

1851   John Manjiro, one of the first Japanese travelers to America arrives. Foreign vessels visit shore in the Ryukyus.

1852   American ship USS Robert Bonn is cast ashore with Chinese laborers.

1853   United States Commodore M.C. Perry arrives in Naha on the Susquehanna and three other ships. Requests are made for free trade with the Ryukyus.

1854   "Treaty of Peace and Amity between the Kingdom of the Ryukyus and the United States." concluded. Russian Admiral Putyatin arrives in the Ryukyus aboard the ship Fregat Pallada. "A Journal of the Perry Expedition to Japan." Published in 1856

The Establishment of the Ryukyu Domain

As Japan opened up and a new government was formed in 1866, the last king of the Ryukyu Kingdom, Sho Tai , had investiture rites performed for his coronation by envoys from China.

In 1871 all of the feudal domains in Japan were abolished and the system of prefectures was established. The Ryukyus were put under the jurisdiction of Kagoshima Prefecture. In 1872 the Meiji government on the mainland summoned envoys and announced that Sho Tai had been appointed King of the Ryukyu Domain.

This was the start of what is called the "Disposition of the Ryukyus".

The Ryukyuan government only understood that this event meant that jurisdiction over the Ryukyus was being transferred from Satsuma to the central government in Tokyo. They did not take notice that the important point of this was the dissolution of the Ryukyu Kingdom.

The Meiji government, wanting to avoid confrontation with the Ryukyuans and Chinese did not immediately implement the dissolution of the domains as it had with the rest of Japan. Instead they took a step by step approach toward the dissolution of the kingdom by naming Sho Tai the "king", not "lord", of a domain.

Dissolution of the Domains and Establishment of the Prefectures

In 1875 the Meiji government formulated policy contained in the edict entitled the "Disposition of the Ryukyus". It conveyed the government's policy of dismantling the Ryukyu Domain and annexing it as Okinawa Prefecture. In the same year it dispatched an official to take charge of the dissolution, Michiyuki Matsuda. His orders were to:

1.Abolish the tributary relationship with China and break off Ryukyuan relations with China.

2.Dispatch young public officials to study the new governmental and educational systems.

3.Reform the administration and institutions under the model of the other prefectures.

4.Establish a military garrison so that the reforms could be conducted without disturbances.

Having received notice of these measures, the Ryukyuan Court, without instituting any countermeasures of their own, simply appealed to the Japanese government to be allowed to continue to conduct the dual tributary relationship with China and Japan it had up until then. Rule in the court was multi-layered and many were simply afraid that by being annexed as part of Japan they would lose land, status and assets.

The Meiji government, deciding that it was unable to understand what the response of the court would be through persuasion, issued an edict authorizing the apprehension of the King.

In March of 1879, after receiving his orders to "abolish the Ryukyu Kingdom and establish Okinawa Prefecture", Matsuda, with police and army units in tow, landed in the Ryukyus and communicated what he was to do to the Ryukyuan court. Through this action all of the land, citizens, and all related documents of the court administration of the former Ryukyuan Royal Court were to be turned over to the Meiji government. Sho Tai, the former king, was given a degree of nobility and ordered to reside in Tokyo. The 500-year rule of the Ryukyu Kingdom was destroyed by these actions.

The Ryukyus and Okinawa

The Chinese used the term Ryukyus in many documents over the course of history. The currently used Chinese characters for the Ryukyus came into use when King Satto of the central Chuzan Kingdom established relations with Ming China in the 14th century.

The current Chinese characters used to designate the prefecture Okinawa came from the name the local people called their own island (Uchina in Okinawan dialect). It was first used in documentation in Japan in the "Tale of the Heike" by Nagato.

There are some historians and who believe the first historical use was a place called "Aji-Naha-to" in the "Todaiwa Joto Seiden." There are also references to Okinawa as "Akina" as well.

The name Okinawa can be found in documents from the Shimazu domain in the 17th century and in Arai Hakuseki's "Nantoshi". In this book Okinawa is written with the current characters and it is therefore said to have been in common use.

When the edict dismantling the Ryukyu Kingdom was issued and the domains were abolished, the prefectural system was established and the Ryukyu Domain was named Okinawa Prefecture because the name Ryukyu came from the Chinese.

The Miyako and Yaeyama Separation from Okinawa

Issues concerning the Ryukyus were not completely solved by dissolving the domains and institution of the prefecture system. China did not recognize this action and there were repeated requests from the Ryukyus for assistance from China.

United States President U. S. Grant was asked by Chinese authorities to help solve the dispute. He held meetings with high Japanese officials such as Ito Hirobumi to try and negotiate. The proposal put forth by the Japanese delegation was that in exchange for recognition of trade and commercial rights within China, similar to those enjoyed by the European countries, the Chinese would take control of the Yaeyama and Miyako Islands. This was the so so-called "Divided Islands / Expanded Treaty" proposal. .

Negotiations ran into difficulties but, with China preoccupied in border disputes with Russia, it agreed to the terms of the treaty anyway.

In February 1881, representatives from both nations were to meet on Ishigaki-jima Island and sign the treaty officially separating the Yaeyama and Miyako Islands and ceding them to China.

However, before formal ratification China experienced internal revolts and fearing the danger of Japanese incursions into Asia refused to conclude the treaty. Also, perhaps because of the influence of repeated requests from Ryukyuans exiled to China, the treaty was shelved.

In 1872 the Ryukyu Domain was established and in 1879 the domain was replaced with the establishment of Okinawa Prefecture. Through this the political process passed from the "Divided Islands / Expanded Treaty" toward what is called the "Disposition of the Ryukyus."

After this, the Japanese advances into Korea led to confrontation with China, which then led to the Sino-Japanese War (1894-1895). With the Japanese victory in this war, Taiwan became a colony of Japan and the "Ryukyu Problem" faded as they were annexed as part of Japan.

Okinawa's Civil Rights Movement

Ancient Customs Preservation Policy

In 1879 when Okinawa Prefecture was established, Naoyoshi Nabeshima, dispatched from the central government, was made governor of the prefecture. After that all the important posts in the Okinawa Prefecture government were entrusted not to Okinawans, but to mainland Japanese. This was the shift to the Yamatoyu, or Japanese world.

The major policy of the Meiji government toward Okinawa was that while changes such as the abolishment of the court bureaucracy and monarchial social positions were carried out, many of the systems were allowed to remain. This was the "Ancient Customs Preservation Policy" and it meant that older systems such as the land allocation, taxation, and local governmental would remain as they had been. This was an attempt to avoid sudden drastic reforms and it was a direction policy took for some time .

There are a number of reasons for this policy including not wanting to invite revolt by the old ruling class in the Ryukyus, the turmoil of the domestic government in the midst of change, and the enormous profit gained by just taking over the existing tax system.

However, the policy was one of the great causes for delays in the modernization of Okinawa.

While the Meiji government offered some guaranteed stipends to the samurai, they were extended only to those registered as descendants of samurai, a small portion of the warrior class. Stipends were not extended to the large majority of low-level unregistered samurai who received very little in the way of economic support during these changes. Many of them were forced to begin new occupations as merchants and farmers. Numerous accounts described the pitiful conditions of the ruined samurai.

The Farmers Movements

When the Meiji government first began implementing the dissolution of the domains, it announced it would reduce the heavy taxation carried out under the old regime. But in reality what the people received under the new system of taxation was the "Preservation of Ancient Customs" policy that was essentially unchanged from the days of the monarchy.

The collapse of the old feudal authority in Shuri however, did most certainly affect the awareness of the people. The common folk, the farmers, began by themselves to insist on guarantees for subsistence.

Anger exploded in many regions at the ruling classes as they used the patently unfair policy to shield themselves. .

On Aguni-jima Island in 1881, farmers, in solidarity, denounced the unjust tax collection of the village officials. In 1883, in Yabu-son village of the Nago district, the farmers demanded the release of the property of the affluent Kugoke houses. Resistance broke out against the unfair policies of the village officials throughout Okinawa. To control the democratic movement brewing in Okinawa, the governor, Michitoshi Iwamura issued a prohibition against protests but the anger of the farmers could not be suppressed.

This type of farmer's protest was directed primarily at the unjust regional officials and taxes and expressed resistance and dissatisfaction with the policy of "Preservation of the Ancient Customs". The movement did not take the form of anything but declarations demanding reform.

The protest movement did have enough influence on the prefectural authorities to get a farmer's representative the right to participate in the budget deliberations in 1888. With the movement to abolish the per capita tax on Miyako-jima Island the protests reached a peak.

The Movement to Abolish the Per Capita Tax

The retention of the per capita tax under the "Preservation of Ancient Customs" policy reduced the residents of Miyako to even deeper poverty. The protest movement that had spread throughout the whole of Okinawa Prefecture sparked a campaign to abolish the head tax in Miyako.

Sugar farming engineer, Seian Gusukuma, and trader Jisaku Nakamura were witness to the suffering and agony of the farmers and were essential in establishing the protest movement in Miyako.

The two headed the list of signatories on the Miyako farmers petition to reduce the number of officials in the regional bureaucracy and abolish the per capita tax. The petition was addressed to the newly appointed Governor Shigeru Narahara . Due to strong resistance from the samurai class the petition was put aside and the result was further an increase in the confrontation between the farmers and the privileged samurai.

The farmers, under the guidance of Gusukuma and Nakamura, submitted the petition again, and because it appeared it would not be accepted, made plans to travel to Tokyo and make a direct appeal to the Imperial Diet. On the way to the capital the samurai and police harassed them but they succeeded in handing the appeal regarding the current status of farmers within Miyako to the Secretary for Home Affairs.

In this way the perseverance of the farmers finally paid off in 1903 when the per capita tax was revoked.

However it should not be overlooked that at the time when they submitted the petition to the 8th Imperial Diet in 1895, Japan was in the midst of the Sino-Japanese War and the central government's belief in the urgent need to modernize Okinawa and integrate the defense of the nation was a reason the government abolished the per capita tax. However, despite this, the fact that the Miyako Farmers Movement did spur the Meiji government and lead the way to a reform of the "Preservation of Ancient Customs" policy makes this worthy of mention due to its effect on the modern history of Okinawa Prefecture.

Noboru Jahana and the Prefectural Government Reform Movement

As the demands to reform the old customs of privilege grew along with the democratic movement in Okinawa, the prefectural authorities were obliged to make moves on the reforms.

When the prefecture's governor during that period, Shigeru Narahara, took office he permitted the reclamation of the Somayama lumber forests managed in common by the farmers under the old royal government and provided relief measures for the poverty stricken lower class samurai families. The push for these reforms came from Noboru Jahana, born in a farming family and one of the first prefectural scholarship students to be sent to the mainland for study.

There were voices heard that this reform would lead to the destruction of the forests and a shortage of resources because of over-harvesting. However, Jahana persuaded the farmers that the cultivation of the land was necessary to bring relief to the poor samurais and if it was made arable and was in a place where it would bring no significant damage to the forests

But the reality of this reform was that it was for the lower-class samurai in name only and the powerful samurai families, Japanese merchants from the mainland, and the top-level officials were given priority in the disposal of the land. The discrimination of the Narahara government toward the Okinawans (Uchinanchu) led Jahana to distrust the leadership and resign his position in the government. He founded a political organization, the Okinawa Club, to oppose the Narahara government. At the same time Jahana developed campaigns for autonomy, suffrage for Okinawans, and reforms of the autocratic style of government.

He persistently attacked the Narahara administration which, together with the old ruling elite, responded by using their political power to oppress the activities of the Okinawa Club. The constant pressure led to the breakup of the organization. Noburu Jahana, penniless and without work, died in misfortune in 1898.

There is much about the work of Jahana and the civil rights movement that is unclear and any evaluations of them remain unsettled. It can be said however that he organized the first political group in Okinawa that centered on the peasants and farmers and had great significance through his attempts to have this reflected in the policies of the prefectural administration.

Reformation of Old Customs and Abolition of Special Institutions

Land Adjustment Practices

The most notable of the reasons for the poverty that Okinawa experienced after the modernization was the retention of the old land allocation system. The land system of Okinawa was a regional allocation system which did not, in principle, allow private ownership of land. The farmers paid tax imposed on the land with tax exceptions given to the richer samurai class and the system was full of inconsistencies.

The movements to abolish the per capita tax and against the unfair tax collection practices by local tax officials came about through the power of the peasant farmers themselves. These movements overlapped with the work of people like Noboru Jahana in the suffrage movement by trying to force reform in land allocation and taxation on the Meiji government.

The Meiji government saw the need for a stable tax system and rational government rule as essential to the transition to a modern capitalist nation and so for these reasons as well the reform of the old systems was an indispensable.

Land adjustments, comparable to the ones carried out in mainland Japan between 1873-1879, were started in Okinawa in 1899 and completed by 1903. The main points of the reform were a recognition of the ownership of the land by the individual farmer originally using that land, that landowners were to be the taxpayers, the abolishment of the per capita tax, and that land tax was to be fixed at 2.5% of the land value. To a certain extent the tax burden was eased but due to increases in the national tax and establishment of new taxes the actual tax burden became heavier as time went on.

However, the land adjustments did have a large impact on the lives of the peasant farmers. Prior to reforms the land was allocated arbitrarily, the crops cultivated were strictly controlled, and tax was made by payment in kind. After the reforms the farmers owned their land and were free to plant what they wanted and tax was regulated. The cultivation of the sole cash crop, sugarcane, spread.

Many farmers suffered under the heavy tax payments and some had to leave their lands and work. Different classes of farmers developed, those without land had no choice either to become employed as tenant farmers or emigrate outside the prefecture or even outside of Japan to find work.

Regional Political Reform and National Government Participation

One more pivotal aspect of the old system preceding the land adjustments was the reorganization of regional governments carried out in 1896. According to this reorganization Okinawa was divided into five counties or districts. These were the Shimajiri, Nakagami, Kunigami, Miyako, and Yaeyama districts and the central urban areas of Naha and Shuri were divided into two wards.. The first three of the districts were assigned district heads and the Sakishima Islands (the Sakishima, Miyako, and Yaeyama Island groups) were assigned island heads. Naha and Shuri were placed under the control of district heads. This clarified the administrative boundaries.

In 1897 the Magiri and Shimabandokoro offices were renamed as government offices and the number of personnel was greatly reduced. . Furthermore, in 1899, a meeting of the island and district assemblies was called whose members were selected by representatives of the islands and districts.

While this was a step toward autonomy, this assembly was not entirely independent of the prefectural authorities. Reforms leading to a more complete regional autonomy would take another 10 years.

In 1908 the jurisdictional suffixes denoted by the words Magiri and Shima were changed to Cho (Town) and Son (Village). Areas previously denoted by Son were changed to Aza. In the following year, 1909, the prefectural assembly was established but there were still many limitations on its authority. It was not until 1920 at the height of the Taisho democracy that the people of Okinawa enjoyed a similar degree of autonomy as the other prefectures of Japan. The activities of Noboru Jahana calling for participation by Okinawa in the National Diet took until 1912 to be implemented. The participation of Miyako and Yaeyama was not allowed until 1919.

The Implementation of a Conscript Military

The Meiji government, aiming at a "Prosperous Nation, Strong Army", modernized the military along the lines of Western military structure and an obligatory military service was instituted with the promulgation of the Military Conscription Ordinance in 1873 .

Planning for the application of this edict in Okinawa began in 1885. By 1896 military service was implemented for primary school teachers and two years later it was applied to the general population. The motivation for conscription of schoolteachers first was to implement an ideological system for indoctrinating loyalty to the emperor in his subjects so that the teachers would then pass on the ideals of military education to the students they taught.

The public servants, educators, and newspaper journalists of Okinawa greeted institution of military conscription as a way the prefecture's citizens could at last be admitted into the circle of citizens of Imperial Japan. The ordinary citizens of Okinawa however saw this in a different light and sought a myriad of ways to avoid military service, from becoming fugitives to feigning disabilities. The number of persons jailed for draft evasion in the first 18 years of conscription was 744 persons.

And those that chose to enter found because many of them spoke no or very little Japanese that there was considerable discrimination against them by mainland Japanese. Having been instilled with the Imperial ideology and as Japanese citizens, there was very little that Okinawans could do to transcend the discrimination they found, except to prove themselves in the battlefield with their blood. The soldiers of Okinawa, unable to change the perceptions of them, finally entered combat in the Russo-Japanese war. The casualty rate for them was around ten percent. Their sacrifice earned them the praise of the Japanese government as true subjects of the Japanese emperor.

Those Okinawans who had turned their backs to the Meiji government over the Sino-Japanese War joined in on the Russo-Japanese War in the spirit of "Chukun- Aikoku" (Loyalty to the Emperor and Patriotism) and started down the way to becoming citizens of the modern Japan.

Education and Academics in Modern Okinawa

The first governor dispatched to Okinawa, Naoyoshi Nabeshima, instituted policies to quickly bring the culture and language into line with standards in Japan. For this reason, Okinawa Teachers' School was established in 1880, the year following the establishment of the prefecture. It was the first such school in Okinawa. As reorganization progressed modern education was introduced through the Okinawa Prefectural elementary and junior high schools.

Initially school attendance was low due to resistance to Japanese rule. In 1887 attendance by girls was permitted. During the Sino-Japanese War attendance remained low at 30% but from the Russo-Japanese War until 1927 attendance steadily rose toward the 99% mark.

By 1900, junior high school education was effected for girls. Public and private schools for girls, vocational schools, and medical training schools were established. However higher education systems, senior high schools and universities were not established and so the leadership level of Okinawan natives did not progress.

The number of young people aiming for careers in academics by traveling to the mainland for higher education gradually increased. Of particular note is the scholar Fuyu Iha who put the highest priority on research concerning the original qualities of Okinawan culture in an age when the rush was to throw aside those practices to conform to Japanese standards.

He protested the discriminatory education against Okinawa in junior high school and continually searched for "a way to live and be Okinawan." After quitting school he went to Tokyo University and studied linguistics, conducting research on the Omoro-soushi, the ancient compilation of ballads and song from the Okinawa and Amami Islands. Not active only in the field of linguistics, he also studied history as well as ethnic studies and conducted comprehensive research on Okinawa throughout his life. Starting with his first book "Koryukyu" (The Ancient Ryukyus) published in 1911, he penned numerous writings on Okinawa related subjects and has since been called the "Father of Okinawan Studies".

Other great scholars from Okinawa included Kanjun Higashionna who wrote "Nanto Fudoki" (Topography of the Southern Islands) as well as

Toso Miyara who conducted thorough linguistic studies of all the dialects in Japan. There were others as well that have left behind an impressive body of research that has stimulated studies on Okinawa.

The Society and Culture of Modern Okinawa

As reforms continued, they brought with them a new and modern Okinawan culture.

In 1893 the first newspaper, The Ryukyu Shimpo, was started and soon many others began publishing as well. While these newspapers all competed for their own development and special interests, they fulfilled a vital role in the debates about government policy and brought new enlightening ways of thinking to the public.

In literature, 1904 saw a Ryukyuan culture and arts renaissance which included the expression of modern viewpoints by such men as Getsujo Iha and many others who wrote for various Japanese literary magazines. Seichu Yamashiro, who had exchanges with the famous poets Akiko and Tekkan Yosano, produced numerous works published within the mainland literary world. Others active in the Taisho period (1912-1926) include Kunio Serei and Sekiho Ikemiyagi and in the Showa period (1926-1988) there was Eikichi Yamazato and Nantestsu Iba. One of the better known of these was Baku Yamanoguchi, who went to Tokyo and lived as a starving artist to write witty poems full of humor and pathos.

In painting, the traditional arts patronized by the old court were preserved and developed but also there was a great influx of Japanese and Western art techniques . Shozan Nakazone, known as an official royal court painter and artist Kakoku Nagamine continued to paint in the traditional styles after the Meiji period began. They also incorporated the new techniques to create their own originality. Seiraku Nishime traveled to Tokyo Art School to learn the techniques of Western painting so that he and his fellow teacher Keijo Higa could pass these new techniques on to the younger generation of painters in Okinawa.

In music the traditional Okinawan music was categorized as Ryukyuan classical music and is the subject of study to this day. Choho Miyara introduced elements of Western music into these compositions and formed a new fusion with the classical Okinawan genre to create popular songs such as "Endo-no Hana" and "Nanta-hama". He was also a teacher of music at a teacher's school.

Performing arts for the public at large were began by those artists who had been schooled as performers for the royal court but had lost their employment when the court was dissolved. They were known as

Shibaishi and through such plays as "Shurijo Hirakewatashi" and operas such as "Tumaiaka" gained reputations as public performers. The older forms of Ryukyuan theater arts such as Ryukyuan Classical Dance and Kumiodori (classical theater) were passed on to the younger performers but it is said there were few opportunities to play them before the public.

Life in Okinawa During the "Cycad Hell"

The Life of Okinawan Citizens During the "Cycad Hell"

After the Russo-Japanese War, Japan experienced a deep economic recession and it was not until the outbreak of WWI in 1914 that things improved because the European powers withdrew from the region leaving Japan in a monopoly position in the Asian market. Economic activity recovered by the export of munitions, iron products and medicines and there was an industrial resurgence in Japan. Okinawa also received the benefits of the upswing by exporting products such as sugar, the profits of which were so great the newly rich were called "Sugar Rich" at the time.

The economic boom during the First World War did not last forever. After WWI the European powers again advanced on the Asian market and Japan's exports plummeted. A domestic surplus of output caused a post-war depression. In Okinawa the price of sugar fell and a wave of depression washed over the islands.

In 1923 the Great Kanto Earthquake and the worldwide effects of the Great Depression caused a chronic economic downturn known as the "Showa Depression" in Japan and this seriously affected the lives of Okinawans as well.

The economic depression that gripped Okinawa from the final years of the Taisho era was named "Sotetsu-jigoku", or "Cycad hell", after a poisonous plant in the palm family the people were forced to process and eat to avoid starvation. Over 70% of the population during this period were farmers and due to the depression, their staples, rice and potatoes, became scarce and they were forced to eat the indigenous plants to survive. Despite the poisonous nature of the plant and the possibility of it causing death if the poison was not completely removed by repeated processing, the impoverished farmers used it to overcome starvation.

Taxes were still collected despite the poverty of the farmers and this combined with the yearly typhoons and occasional droughts made life hell for the Okinawans. Many were forced to sell relatives and others migrated overseas or to mainland Japan in search of work.

Emigration and Employment Overseas

As Okinawa is an island prefecture with scarce arable land , the poor of Okinawa sought a means of escape by overseas emigration.

In 1899 the first 26 immigrants from Okinawa were dispatched to Hawaii under the efforts of Kyuzo Toyama and in the seven years after, over 4670 joined them in their immigration, most of them to Hawaii. The Okinawans seeking to escape the Cycad Hell occupied over 10% of the Japanese who immigrated in the years between 1923 and 1930.

The funds sent from overseas back to Okinawa gave significant and much needed support for their families and aided the economy of Okinawa as a whole. While there were some great success stories, most of those who went to work overseas had to endure hardships while continuing to work.

In addition to those working overseas, there were many Okinawans who moved to the mainland to find work. Most of the immigrants to the mainland settled in the Kobe-Osaka region and worked in the spinning and weaving industries. Many worked in appalling conditions and were humiliated by the discrimination against Okinawans.

Many formed organizations and associations of Okinawans as peer support seeking to raise the appalling living standards of Okinawan workers. They survived and got stronger.

Okinawa Social Movement

In the capitalist but underdeveloped Okinawa, the socialist theories of class struggle and labor movement spread from people that had gone to the mainland of Japan to work.

In the early 1900's the ideas of socialism spread to the educators and intelligentsia and on other levels of society. Disputes between tenant farmers and landowners erupted frequently.

In 1926 leaders of the mainland Socialist movement formed the Okinawa Seinen Domei (Okinawa Youth Alliance) and coordinated a strike of the labor unions in various professions. In the first general election in Japan in 1928 (only males 25 and older were franchised), the socialist leaders ran in the election and the activities of the party picked up.

The student movements and teacher unions were also very active. Okinawan citizens attending university in Tokyo and senior high teachers' school intensified their activities and more than a few were dismissed or punished. Around 1930 the teacher's unions were formed on Yaeyama and the main island of Okinawa.

The response of the authorities to the intensified activities of the socialists was to exert control by using special police units that began an unfair crackdown on various socialist movement activities. In the middle 1930's many student and movement leaders were jailed and were forcibly deported from Okinawa. By 1940 the social movements in Okinawa were facing one of their most difficult periods.

The Dialect Controversy and Imperialist Education

Together with the end of the Sino-Japanese War and the wave of modernization, there were moves to bring the culture and manners of the Okinawans into line with that of mainland Japan. In the first decade of the Showa era (1926-1988) this activity increased, even to the extent of having people change the pronunciation of the characters in their names to sound more Japanese.

The pending issue of rigid enforcement of the use of standard Japanese intensified as nationalist sentiment grew. In 1940 the prefectural authorities promoted enforcement of the use of standardized Japanese thorough such measures as coercion and prohibition as they took steps to "Eradicate Okinawan Dialect". The presence of such people as the Japan Folk Craft Association's Muneyoshi Yanagi (Soetsu Yanagi) in Okinawa who criticized the enforcement as going too far, ignited debates about dialect both in and outside the prefecture.

This controversy did not result in any definite conclusion but the enforcement of a unified system in Japan only got more coercive as Japan began the road to militarism and war. When the battle for Okinawa began the Japanese army regarded anyone using Okinawan dialect as a spy and used severe pressure on those who used it. During the battle there incidents where the use of dialect resulted in tragedy for those who used it.

The viewpoints of Yanagi and others began to have more influence after the war when reflection on the problems caused by contempt for Okinawans and the idea that Okinawa could simply be made to follow Japan. Reflection on these lead to reaffirmation of the richness of Okinawan culture.

The Battle of Okinawa

Evacuations and the 10/10 Air Raid

From the first days of the Asia- Pacific war, Okinawa was fortified as the location of airbases and as the frontline in the defense of mainland Japan. Land and farms were forcibly expropriated throughout Okinawa and the Imperial Japanese Army began the construction of airbases.

In 1944, the 32nd Army of Okinawa was established and fighting units of the military were dispatched to the Okinawa Islands and the Sakishima Islands (Sakishima Island and the Miyako and Yaeyama

Island groups). In the areas to which they were dispatched, the local schools and houses were used as garrisons and the local farmers were required to provide logistical supplies from their own food and domesticated animals.

As the war entered its final stage, the fall of Saipan Island, home to so many immigrants from Okinawa, had a deep impact on the people of Okinawa. Not only sorrow because of the loss of fellow countrymen but also dread knowing that the next target of the advance would be Okinawa.

In order to fight a protracted war using Okinawa as a frontline, the young, old, and infirm were evacuated from the prefecture. The Japanese government made plans to evacuate 80,000 Okinawans to mainland Japan and 20,000 to Taiwan but because of reluctance to go to an unknown land and the presence of enemy ships in the seas near Okinawa, the plans were not fully implemented. Incidents such as the torpedoing of the Tsushima Maru, which was carrying 1700 passengers, including 800 school children , heightened the anxiety surrounding evacuation considerably.

However, after the 10/10 Air Raid attacks on October 10, 1944, the number of those willing to chance evacuation increased greatly.

The 10/10 Air Attack, so called because it took place in the tenth month on the tenth day was a massive aerial bombardment of the entire Nansei Island region by the U. S. Military. Attacks were made on the Amami-jima islands in the north to Ishigaki-jima Island in the south and Daito-jima Island in the east. In Naha City the fierce attack burned out 90% of the buildings in the city and many priceless cultural treasures of the Ryukyuan Kingdom were lost. The air attack consisted of 1400 aircraft and inflicted 600 deaths and 700 injuries.

The Start of the Battle of Okinawa

In Okinawa, starting in 1943, military drills taught in the junior high school were intensified. . In July of the same year Prime Minister Hideki Tojo visited Okinawa, in November nurse training for girl students was begun and the student mobilization system was fully established.

After the air raids of October 10, 1945, mobilization of the students intensified, evacuation of students was no longer permitted and a system was prepared so the schools could give complete support to the armed forces. In February of 1945, male teachers and students from the middle and teaching schools were organized into the Imperial Blood and Iron Corps and the women and girls were organized into the Himeyuri Nurse Corps as nurses attached to the Japanese Haebaru infantry field hospital on the battlefields.

After the first massive bombing on September 10, 1944, the beginning of the New Year saw further intensification of the air attacks by the US forces and the conquest of Okinawa was only a matter of time.

On March 26, 1945 the U.S. forces landed on the Kerama Islands. The dreadful ground war was begun.

Most of the units stationed in the Kerama Islands were marine volunteers and special attack units, there were hardly any infantry troops there at all . Due to the sudden landing by U.S. forces on Kerama, the Japanese troops fled to hide in caves in the middle mountainous part of the island. After resisting as hard as they were able, the volunteer forces were completely crushed. The civilians were given orders directly and indirectly to commit suicide to avoid capture. Many civilians, with no place to escape to and in ignorant fear of the American troops, gathered together and killed themselves and their relatives and children in group suicides. In the Kerama islands the death toll from these group suicides was 329 people for Tokashiki-jima Island, 171 persons on Zamami-jima Island, and on Geruma-jima Island it was 53 people.

Progress of the Battle of Okinawa

On April 1, 1945, U.S. military forces landed at Yomitan, Kadena and Chatan in the middle part of the main island of Okinawa without experiencing any resistance or casualties. They immediately occupied two former airfields of the Japanese forces. The main reason for the lack of resistance was that the transfer of troops to other locations had left them short in Okinawa and the Japanese had to shift their strategy from a shoreline defense to plans for a protracted holding action. The strategy was that if the U.S. forces could be delayed in their conquest of Okinawa, the mainland of Japan would have more time to become sufficiently prepared for a decisive battle there.

On April 2, the day after landing, the U.S. forces reached the eastern seacoast and divided the island in two. By April 20th they had substantially effected occupation of the entire northern area. The civilians hiding in the mountainous areas, weakened by malaria and starvation, had not only the bullets of the U. S. forces to fear, but also needed to protect themselves from the plundering, torture and massacres committed by the remaining Japanese soldiers.

The battles up in the northern part of the island around the airfield on Ie-jima Island were particularly fierce. In the six days of intense fighting many civilians as well as soldiers lost their lives. Over 100 of the civilians died in group suicides.

In the mid-southern areas the defending Japanese forces attacked the U.S. forces in heated battles for a few days but after losing over half of their fighting units suffered complete defeat. On May 27, 1945 the units of the Japanese army defending Okinawa retreated from their underground headquarters in Shuri to Mabuni in the southern part of the island. Finding the caves already occupied by civilian refugees, the Japanese forces ejected them, requisitioned the refugee's supplies and in some cases executed them.

As the Japanese forces retreated in battle from their airfield in Oroku, Rear Admiral Minoru Ota, after noting the bravery of the Okinawans supporting the Imperial Navy units there sent a telegram saying , "Thus fought the Okinawans, and I ask you to consider these prefectural citizens as meriting future reward." After this he committed suicide and the army was crushed.

The Japanese forces retreated to the southernmost tip and after losing the final battle on June 22 (some accounts say June 23), the commander, Lt. General Mitsuru Ushijima and Chief of Staff, Isamu Cho, committed suicide and all organized resistance was finished. Pockets of resistance continued to fight the U.S. forces, even after the

Battle of Okinawa was finished on July 2, 1945. It was not until September 2, 1945 that the head of the remaining Japanese forces on the island signed formal surrender.

War on the Sakishima and Other Island Groups

During the Battle of Okinawa, the other islands where the U.S. forces did not land such as on the Sakishima Islands (Sakishima, Miyako-jima Island, and the Yaeyama Island group) also experienced great sacrifices.

On Sakishima there was considerable damage from the aerial bombardment of the U.S. and British navies but, the most serious damage was caused by lack of food and malaria.

On Yaeyama, the people were forced to leave their homes and go into the mountainous areas. 3,647 people, about 11% of the population, contracted and died of malaria. The six thousand residents of Miyako-jima Island had over three thousand troops stationed there and suffered extreme food shortages and malaria.

On Izena-jima Island on the northern coast of the Okinawa mainland , three U.S. servicemen cast ashore were executed under orders by Japanese soldiers, who then went on to kill the nearby villagers. The islands of Iheya-jima and Aguni-jima had no Japanese troops stationed there and the U.S. forces landed smoothly and there were effectively no great losses of life. Residents were able to surrender smoothly to U. S. forces as a result. The presence or absence of Japanese troops determined the extent of the casualties suffered by the civilian residents. On the small island Sesoko-jima, on the north coast of Okinawa, the residents, fearing the casualties caused by the presence of Japanese troops, repelled the Japanese soldiers that had crossed over to escape from the main island.

The presence of bomber base on Tsuken-jima in the Nakagusuku Gulf meant that this area became one of intense fighting. On Tonaki-jima Island, communications were cut with the mainland of Okinawa, residents were forced to endure starvation until the news of the end of the war reached there in the middle of September.

Post-War Okinawa

On August 15, 1945 Japan signed the Potsdam Declaration, ending World War Two after fighting for fifteen years. The Allied forces occupied Japan and the Nansei Islands were put under U.S. military rule.

The United Nations was founded centering on the nations that had won in WWII, but a new kind of international tension arrived with the

Cold War competition between the West, allies of the United States, and the East, centered on the Soviet Union. With the intensification of the Cold War and the establishment of socialist governments in China and North Korea, the U.S. came to regard the geographic position of Okinawa as strategically important and the basis for a long term rule over the islands became a fixed policy.

In 1949, with long-term rule in mind, the military government implemented economic reconstruction and democratic government, consolidated the military facilities, began planning for permanent bases and granted a certain degree of self-autonomy to the residents of Okinawa. In December of the following year, the strong direct government of the U.S. Navy was replaced by the United States Civil Administration of the Ryukyu Islands (USCAR) but overall control remained unchanged and was retained by the military.

In 1951 the San Francisco Peace Treaty and the U.S. Japan Security Treaty were concluded and Japan regained independence, but the islands of Okinawa remained under the authority of the U.S. Government. As Japan joined the other nations of the West, Okinawa became a stronghold in the fight against the communists of China, North Korea, and the Soviet Union.

With the international situation such as it was, the bases on Okinawa underwent full-scale strengthening. In 1953 The U.S. Civil Administration began land expropriations in support of the strengthening of the bases. The Okinawan resistance to the land requisitions was strong, igniting an "island-wide struggle" whose momentum continued to gather steam under the "Reversion Movement."

In 1965 Japanese Prime Minister Eisaku Sato visited Okinawa and began to press for the return of Okinawa to Japan. Okinawa's reversion to Japan was realized on May15, 1972. Still 25 years since the reversion to Japan, Okinawa, occupying only 1% of the land area of Japan, is the location of 75% of the U.S. military bases in Japan. There remain many issues concerning the bases.

Defeat and U.S. Occupation

The Start of U.S. Occupation

In March 1945 the U.S. forces that landed on the Kerama Islands issued the Nimitz Declaration suspending all the political rights of the Japanese Imperial Government and declared the Nansei Islands under the jurisdiction of the Untied States Navy. From that date, Okinawa was severed from Japan for 27 years until the reversion on May 15,

1972. Okinawa experienced a very different kind of postwar life than did the mainland of Japan.

On April 1, 1945 the U.S. forces landed in the Hija area of Yomitan-son and began to establish military rule throughout the Nansei Islands.

In August of the same year Japan signed the Potsdam Declaration, ending the war. On that same day, at the invitation of the U.S. military government, Okinawan leaders from the internment camps held meetings in Ishikawa City in the central area of mainland Okinawa. This was the first democratic assembly of residents in postwar Japan. The result of that meeting was the formation of the "Okinawa Advisory Council." Mr. Koshin Shikiya was chosen to head the assembly. On April of the following year the Council became the Okinawa Civil Government, thus the Okinawan Legislature was established.

However, the military government appointed all the governor and assembly members. After that rule shifted from the U.S. Navy to the U.S. Army, and later on to the U.S. Civil Administration, but real power rested with the U.S. military.

Various Postwar

The Okinawan War Memorial Day is on June 23 , the day of the suicide of Lt. Gen. Mitsuru Ushijima, commander of the 32nd Imperial Japanese Army. (Ushijima's suicide actually took place the day before on June 22nd.). But it was not the day the Battle of Okinawa ended. Confrontations between the United States military and Imperial Japanese forces continued after June 23rd.

The U.S. forces announced the end of the battle on July 2, 1945, but pockets of resistance from isolated Imperial Japanese troops continued. The strategies for getting them under control continued even after the surrender of Japan on August 15, 1945. As a result, substantial conflicts occurred until the formal surrender of the remaining Japanese forces on September 7, 1945.

In June of the same year, even as the battles were still being conducted on Okinawa, the first schools opened in the internment camps of each region and classes were being taught. Newspapers were published from the camps as well. In the camps, food and provisions were offered free of charge and at the same time Okinawans began to learn about the prosperity of Americans and about democracy.

On islands where the U.S. forces made no landings during the Battle of Okinawa, such as on the Yaeyama Islands, the residents began to build democratic organizations by themselves. But in December U.S. forces were stationed there and the rule of the military government began.

The Start of Postwar Government

The U.S. military government took note of the achievements of the Okinawa Advisory Council and in April of 1946 renamed it the Okinawa Civil Government and appointed Koshin Shikiya as governor of the civil government. They also established a legislature and appointed representatives. The political and administrative framework was made with the forceful intention of the U.S. military government. It was said that The U.S. military was the cat and Okinawa was the mouse. Another saying at the time was "The mouse can only play in the range the cat allows," and the civil rights of the residents were fairly confined.

In 1950 four Gunto districts were created; the Amami Islands Gunto, the Okinawa Islands Gunto, the Miyako Islands Gunto, and the Yaeyama Islands. Elections were held and governors were selected, but the wishes of the Okinawans were not at all reflected in the policies of the military government.

During this time, the U.S. military, having separated its occupation of Okinawa from that of mainland Japan, did not initiate any clear- cut policies due to the opposition of the U.S. State Department to permanent U.S. Bases on Okinawa. For this reason, Okinawa was termed the "forgotten island", progress was held in stasis, and confusion on the island continued.

In 1946, the postwar constitution was promulgated on the Japanese mainland and democratization of the nation began under occupation. However, in Okinawa the residents suffered through difficulties obtaining food, high- handedness of the U.S. soldiers, and restrictions on freedoms such as speech, assembly, and the right to self-government. In the midst of these conditions, Okinawans, together with those repatriated from the mainland, began the movement to expand autonomy .

In May 1947, the "Okinawa Kensetsu Kondankai," the first postwar island-wide political assembly, was held and a petition was submitted to the Okinawa Civil Administration Governor concerning demands for the establishment of an assembly that would reflect the will of the Okinawan people, an end to corruption, and a more equitable and adequate supply distribution system. Taking this opportunity, the Okinawa Democratic Union, the Okinawa People's Party, and the Okinawa Socialist Party were established. The military government recognized the local municipal elections for the assemblies and village and city mayors, but was unenthusiastic about the recognition of the election of a governor and an Okinawan assembly. Far from accepting, the reaction, the military authorities were autocratic and there were interruptions of supply deliveries, price hikes, and dissolution of the Okinawa Legislature in an attempt at suppression. This confrontation led to the growth of demands for self-government among the Okinawans.

Life under the U.S. Occupation

Around October1945, permission was granted to move out of the internment camps and back into the villages and towns. But when residents returned to their villages, some found their land had been requisitioned as munitions or supply depots and they had no place to go.

The prewar system of municipalities and jurisdictions was revived, but it entailed starting from zero. Among the residents who were trying hard just to get food and supplies, the "fruits of war," black markets in stolen goods started forming and there were more than a few instances where persons stealing were shot at by U.S. troops.

In the middle part of 1946 there was still no currency available, so goods were bartered. There were several currency exchanges that occurred after this time but to prevent the inflation caused by the influx of Japanese yen, the military government introduced the B Yen currency, which provided a start for economic activities.

However, commodity prices, wages, and salaries were controlled so there were no free exchange transactions. This was when the black markets and smuggling goods became a major activity. In a life with so many restrictions, the residents of Okinawa constructed Sanshin (Okinawan samisen) from whatever was available, such as tin cans and string. They played and sang songs, prayed to their village gods, and tried to reconstruct Okinawa.

USCAR and the Struggle for Autonomous Rights

The Policy of Maj. Gen. Sheets and the Treaty of San Francisco

Early relief funding provided by the GARIOA (Government and Relief in Occupied Areas) was taken over by the LARA Program (Licensed Agencies for Relief in Asia) in 1949. This was the start of economic recovery in Okinawa.

The U.S. military placed Major General Joseph R. Sheets in command of the U.S. Directive Administration for Okinawa (RYCOM) as governor to oversee the restoration of order in the government. General Sheets planned for the permanent rule and construction of U. S. Military bases on Okinawa and accomplished a number of policies during his time. The policies he advocated were received by the Okinawans kindly and his term in office was widely regarded as "The Good Government of Sheets".

The first of his policies implemented as governor was the reorganization of the jumble of military facilities and facilities construction with a high degree of order and efficiency. In the next set of policies he set out to accomplish increasing the extent of social welfare systems. The third set of policies was the public recognition of self-rule, the reduction of military government on each of the island groups, and the implementation of elections for governor and members of an island-wide legislature. In December 1950, the American Far East Command issued orders for dissolution of the U. S. Military Government and the establishment of the United States Civil Administration of the Ryukyu Islands (USCAR) .

In September of 1951, representatives from fifty-two nations gathered at U.S. invitation in San Francisco and opened a conference on the proposed peace treaty with Japan. Japan called for a universal peace treaty with all nations that it had fought with in WWII, including the Soviet Union and China. Prime Minister Shigeru Yoshida participated in the conference which resulted in the conclusion of a peace treaty with forty-eight of the participating countries. This was the San Francisco Peace Treaty.

In the 3rd article of the treaty, it stated the conditions of U.S. right to rule the Okinawa and Amami Islands. In three months time over 70% of the legal voters in Okinawa signed petitions in objection to this, but this was disregarded by both the Japanese and U.S. governments. Simultaneously, Japan concluded the Japan - U.S. Security Treaty. On April 28, 1952 both treaties took effect and Japan regained its independence.

Okinawa was separated from Japan and became the "Keystone of the Pacific," assuming an important and strategic place in U.S. policy in Asia.

The Establishment of the Government of the Ryukyus

In 1950, in the Gunto Island district governor elections, many of those elected had waged campaigns stressing the idea of reversion to Japan. In the reforms carried out within the political parties as a result of the elections, the promotion of reversion to Japan became part of the basic party platform of the Okinawa Socialist Masses Party (Shadaito).

After the election of the Gunto district governors, the U.S. government changed the administration of the islands from the military government to the three tiered United States Civil Administration of the Ryukyu Islands (USCAR). This federal system consisted of the Central Government, the Gunto Governments and the municipal city and village jurisdictions.

The U.S. by now had become aware of the reversion sentiments of the Gunto district governments and in April of 1951 established the Provisional Central Government to protect its legislative, judicial and administrative rights until a more permanent Central Government could be formed. With the appearance of the Provisional Central Government the Gunto governments became governments in name only.

In March of 1952 the residents of Okinawa voted in majority for candidates that were promoting the reversion to Japan in a direct election of the legislature. The U.S. Civil Administration sensed an impending crisis and, on April 1, appointed Shuhei Higa as the first chief executive of the Government of the Ryukyus Islands. The Gunto governments, elected by the people of Okinawa with their hopes in mind, were disbanded.

Okinawa as a Strategic Base

In Okinawa in the 1950's, the base expansion reached a peak of activity , a symbol of the rising tensions between the U.S. and the Soviet Union. Around the time the Treaty of San Francisco was concluded and the leased land contracts for the military bases advanced as well. Before that the land expropriated for military bases was used free of charge, but starting in 1946, the land ownership projects re-established land ownership and there were demands from the landowners for compensation.

With the conclusion of the treaty, the basis for the use of land without payments no longer applied and the establishment of leases became a necessity for the U.S. military. The U.S. Civil Administration promised to pay rent dated back to 1950. However, the rates were so low the resistance to them was extreme.

USCAR's expectations to conclude the leasing agreements were not met so it issued land acquisition procedures in April of 1953. Residents who refused to vacate expropriated land were forcibly evicted at bayonet point and the houses were bulldozed over.

This was how the large U.S. military bases appeared in Okinawa. The people who had lost their land were employed on the bases, but the industrial base was weak and the economy became distorted and consumption oriented.

The Price Report and the Island-wide Struggles

In March of 1954 the U.S. Civil Administration indicated it would issue land rents in one ten-year lump sum payment. In response to this, the elected legislature, in keeping with the will of the Okinawan residents, passed a resolution containing the "Four Principles of Land Protection." This was the start of island-wide protests.

The U.S. Civil Administration regarded the principles as unrealistic, ignored them, and continued their forcible expropriation of land. Increasingly resolute Okinawan resistance led the Government of the Ryukyus to dispatch a delegation in May 1955 to Washington to present the "Four Principles" directly to the American government. In response to the submission of the appeal from the delegation from Okinawa, a U.S. House of Representative committee dispatched a survey group headed by Senator Price to Okinawa.

The results of Senator Price's survey were presented to the U.S. Congress in the following year. It contained no mention of the Okinawan desire for reversion to Japan. It also contained details of the conditions of the U.S. rule in Okinawa and spoke of the desirability for a long term U.S. military presence in Okinawa. The report was a bitter disappointment to the Okinawans and throughout the islands groups gathered in protests. 1956 was the year when the "Island-wide Struggle" was ignited.

Toward these protests USCAR issued an off-limits order to military personnel forbidding their people access to civilian areas. This inflicted economic damage on Okinawa. As a result the Government of the Ryukyus recognized the use of land for the bases, the U.S. Civil Administration promised to award fair value for land use and the matter was finally settled

The Rise of the Popular Movement and Reversion

Damage from the Bases and Okinawan Human Rights

On June 30, 1959 a U.S. military jet crashed on Miyamori Elementary School in Ishikawa City and was reported worldwide as one of the worst tragedies in the history of aviation. Seventeen people were killed, eleven of them children, and 121 people were gravely injured. Twenty-five houses were burned. The U.S. military made a definite promise to compensate for the accident but it took them nearly three years to finally give payment.

During this period there were numerous incidents where the human rights of the Okinawans were disregarded by the U.S. military. There were also many problems relating to the legal judgements regarding crimes and accidents. Many of the accused were found not guilty and even in cases where guilt was established, perpetrators were sent back to the U.S. where the execution of sentences was obscured. Okinawan residents were forced to swallow the injustices.

There was further damage to the environment from live-fire exercises, pollution from nuclear-powered submarines, contamination of water supplies, wells, and soil from effluent waste from the bases. These became daily occurrences.

Under the rule of the U.S. military, the American military received all priority and the human rights of the Okinawans were ignored. The economic prosperity of the 1960's in Okinawa brought by the military bases was paid for in the danger to the lives of the Okinawans and the disregard for their basic rights.

The Rise of the People

On April 28, 1960 the Okinawa Teacher's Association, the Okinawa Prefecture Association of Youth Groups, and the Union of Government Employees of Okinawa acted as go-betweens in the organization of a nonpartisan group, The Okinawa Reversion Council, devoted to issues regarding the return of Okinawa to the mainland of Japan. Following this, activities for reversion were conducted but the U.S. Civil Administration enacted no changes in their rule over Okinawa.

If a situation occurred that was not to the convenience of USCAR, which held the real power within Okinawa, a decree or announcement was made and the demands of the residents were ignored or denied. In 1963 the High Commissioner, Lt. General Paul W. Caraway caused a stir with his pronouncements on the "Myth of Okinawan Autonomy" and the direct control of the U.S. Civil Administration over Okinawa came into view.

Under the rule of such a Hicom, dissatisfaction with the lack of will shown by the Government of the Ryukyus spread to all levels of Okinawan society. Civic activism shook the entirety of the Okinawa Islands with the aim of a return to Japan. The movement became the focus of international attention.

With the intensification of the Vietnam War in the 1960's, the U.S. military came under increasing criticism internationally and this caused great change. U.S. President Lyndon Johnson was pressed to cease the bombing of North Vietnam and the issue of an Okinawan reversion to Japan was taken up between the governments of Japan and the United States.

The Development of the Popular Movement

In the 1960's the land disputes had settled down to a certain degree, but issues regarding the bases continued to weigh heavily on Okinawans. The residents of Okinawa came to the recognition that these problems were derived from rule by a foreign country and the desire developed to abolish this domination, and return to Japan under it's constitution of peace. This spurred the movement toward reversion. Through this movement the struggle to force withdrawal of the "Twin Education Bills" and the establishment of direct election for the office of Chief Executive of the Government of the Ryukyus developed. The "Twin Education Bills" were aimed at controlling the civic activism of teachers.

The bills were entitled the "Regional Education District Public Employee Law" and the "Special Law for Public Employees in Education." Similar laws had already been effected in the mainland of Japan. They included the enactment of regulations on the political activity of educators and were taken as an attempt to smash the reversion movement that included the teaching unions. Resistance to these measures sprung up.

However, the power of the conservative Democratic Party was squarely behind passage of the bills and the debate split the unity of the Okinawans into two.

After numerous attempts to have the bill brought to a vote the conservatives forced a vote during the February Plenary session of the legislature. Over twenty thousand attended a demonstration in front of the Legislature building in support of the teachers and the bill was withdrawn. With the backdrop of the mass demonstration outside the Legislature, the minority party of the Legislature got withdrawal of the bill and received great praise from all quarters.

Close of the Return to Japan Movement and Okinawan Reversion

When Japanese Prime Minister Eisaku Sato visited Okinawa in 1965 he stated that "The postwar era will not end so long as Okinawa is not returned." However, the terms of reversion as advocated bilaterally by Japan and the U.S. and those sought by the Okinawan people were quite divergent in nature.

The Okinawan Reversion movement began to resist the rule of a foreign nation and as civic activism to unify with their ethnic group. After the protests against the "Twin Education Bills" in the latter half of the 1960's, the struggle, which had begun by waving the Hinomaru flag of Japan as a symbol, shifted emphasis for unification with their ethnic group toward being anti-war and pacifist.

In 1968 in the elections for the Chief Executive of the Government of the Ryukyus, Chobyo Yara, a candidate that stressed "immediate, unconditional, and complete reversion" soundly beat out the other candidate and won the office of Chief Executive . The defeated Junji Nishime had also stressed unification with Japan. Also in 1970, the enactment of a bill in the Japanese Diet allowed elected representatives from Okinawa participation in the Diet. The resulting election saw victory for the Reformist candidates and indicated the hopes of the Okinawan people in a removal of the military bases from Okinawa.

In November of 1969, the talks between Japanese Prime Minister Sato and U.S. President Nixon resulted in a joint declaration of a "non-nuclear Okinawa, one of parity with Japan, and reversion in 1972". Opposition to the details of the agreement caused widespread protest among the Okinawan people.

Okinawan Culture under U.S. Military Rule

Due to the fierceness of the Battle of Okinawa, many of the superb cultural legacies created during the Ryukyu Kingdom Era were lost or destroyed. Gathering up the scattered and lost pieces of this cultural heritage became the start of Okinawa's cultural reconstruction.

The U.S. military expressed understanding of the collection of cultural artifacts. The residents of Shuri collected the cultural properties scattered about and in 1946 opened the Shuri City Folk Museum, which became the Shuri Museum the following year. In 1945 the U.S. military opened the Okinawa Display Hall in the Higashionna area of Ishikawa City . The following year this became the Higashionna Folk Museum.

In May 1953 these museums were consolidated into the Museum of the Government of the Ryukyu Islands, which at present has become the Okinawa Prefectural Museum. In the 1950's the cultural properties were restored and reconstructed. The Sunu-hiyan Utaki Ishimon Stone Gate and Shureimon Gate in Shuri were reconstructed.

The U.S. Civil Administration also established the Ryukyu Cultural Hall and the Ryukyu Friendship Center as facilities for exchange between the Okinawan people and Americans. The educational system was started in the internment camps after the war but a 6-year elementary, a 3-year junior high and 3 year senior high school system was implemented in 1948. In 1950 the University of the Ryukyus was founded on the site of the ruined Shuri Castle.

The field of literature began again. Taking themes from their lives resisting the rule of a foreign nation, writers Tatsuhiro Oshiro and Mineo Higashi both won the prestigious Akutagawa Prize for Literature. In the areas of music and the performing arts, Ryukyuan music and Ryukyuan Dance experienced a great resurgence. The youth of Okinawa took to the jazz and rock they heard from the servicemen on the bases and a new generation of active musicians was fostered. The mixture of jazz, rock, and traditional Okinawan folk songs resulted in the birth of Okinawan Music.

The Phases of Pre-Reversion Okinawa

In November 1968, immediately after the elections for Chief Executive called for by massive public activism, a number of base-related accidents occurred. First, a U.S. B-52 bomber crashed on take-off from Kadena Airfield and then a munition carrier crashed and overturned nearby. Okinawa during that period was an embarkation point for U.S. troops heading to Vietnam and the B-52s routinely took off for bombing runs to Vietnam. This was the context in which the Okinawan mass movements for pacifism and against war developed.

In 1970, at year's end, an accident occurred where a car driven by a U.S. soldier struck an Okinawan crossing an intersection in Nakanomachi, Koza City (Okinawa City). Residents, feeling resentment at the frequency of these incidents and the unfair handling of such cases, exploded with anti-U.S. sentiment and rioted. Over seventy cars were burned that night in the so-called Koza Riot.

This affair, occurring as it did in a town dependent on the U.S. military bases and by people regarded as obedient by the military authorities, came as a big shock to the American military. It also influenced the negotiations for reversion of Okinawa that were taking place between Japan and the United States.

The talks for reversion involving governments of both countries ignored the Okinawan people's hope for a non-nuclear island of peace and continued laying the foundation for a continued base presence on Okinawa. The Reversion Council decried the "Agreement between Japan and the United States concerning the Ryukyu Islands and the Daito Islands" and carried out general strikes throughout Okinawa.

Without concern for these events, the governments of Japan and the United States concluded the agreement with a joint signing in Tokyo and Washington in June 1971. The decisions made regarding the conditions of reversion ignored the demands of the Okinawan people. Okinawans, wanting a revision of the reversion agreement before ratification in the Diet, staged a massive demonstration calling for re-negotiation. However, despite the petitions brought to Tokyo by Chief

Executive Yara the reversion agreement was forcibly voted on in the Diet.

The New Life of Okinawa

Rebirth of Okinawa Prefecture

In January 1972 Japanese Prime Minister Sato and American President Nixon held consultations and decided on May 15, 1972 as the day of reversion.

The Government of the Ryukyus established the "People's Council on Restoration Issues" to advise the Chief Executive. They studied summaries of the reversion policies of both Japan and America. Chief Executive Chobyo Yara received the report and petitioned both governments, finally writing a petition submitted to an extraordinary session of the Diet entitled the "Recommendations Regarding Reversion" emphasizing the theme of "immediate, unconditional, and complete reversion." On the day of submission of the recommendations a vote was forced on the reversion agreement and it was approved by the Diet.

On May15, 1972, after twenty-seven years of U.S. rule the islands of Okinawa reverted back to Japan. The terms of reversion were a far cry from the hopes of the residents of Okinawa, but, return to the sovereignty of the nation of Japan but reversion was none the less accomplished.

To start the new life of Okinawa Prefecture the Japanese government held commemorative services in Tokyo and Okinawa. The Tokyo ceremonies were held at the Budokan and Prime Minister Sato, U.S. Vice-President Agnew , and Lt. Gen. J. P. Lampert were in attendance. The ten thousand people there celebrated the new life of Okinawa Prefecture..

In Okinawa Prefecture the ceremonies included an address by Governor Yara, a man who had experienced the full bitterness involved with this day because of the various issues surrounding the reversion, including those of the U.S. military bases on Okinawa.

The Okinawa Reversion Council, which had promoted the reversion effort, opened a general meeting in Naha's Yogi Koen Park on the day of reversion and adopted a resolution opposing the reversion. On the other hand, the Okinawa Executive committee organized a celebratory meeting in Naha City on the night before the reversion

Special Reversion Measures and Life of the Prefectural Citizens

Life for the citizens of Okinawa changed greatly after reversion to mainland Japan. One of the first things was the currency shift from dollars to yen. The dollar was low against the yen at the time of reversion. The Japanese government decided that was a loss of profit for the Okinawans and promised to exchange dollars at the rate of 360 yen to the dollar, with the difference in the real rate to be compensated by the Japanese government. But, because of various related problems and because of price hikes, consumer prices rose 14.5% in one month.

In order to smooth the change in the economy of Okinawa after twenty-seven years of separate development from the economic and political system of the mainland, the government devised the Special Reversion Measures. According to these measures, the Okinawa Development Agency was to formulate plans every ten years for Okinawa's promotion and development in order to correct the disparities between the mainland and Okinawa. This public fund was established to maintain the roads, harbors and agriculture, and gradually the income of the prefecture's citizens grew.

As projects commemorating the reversion, in November 1972 the Planting Festival to Commemorate Reversion was held, in May of 1973 the Okinawa Special National Athletic Meet (the Wakanatsu Games) were held, and starting in July of 1975 for half a year, the Okinawa International Ocean Exposition was held.

On July 30,1978 the traffic patterns changed to the left to meet Japanese standards in the "People to the right, Cars to the Left" campaign.

Keywords in Postwar Okinawa

Yaka Horyo Shuyou-jo (Yaka POW Camp)

Located in the Yaka district of Kin-cho village, the internment camp was a large-scale facility for Imperial Japanese Army prisoners after the war. There were 7,000 prisoners housed here, including 5,000 Japanese troops. The remaining were Koreans and Okinawan- born soldiers.

Okinawa Shijun-kai (Okinawa Advisory Council)

Established by the U.S. Military Government, the Advisory Council was an intermediate organization paving the way for the establishment of the central government. There were 15 members consisting mostly of educators and media people. Koshin Shikiya was chosen as council chair.

Okinawa Min Seifu (Okinawa Civil Government)

In 1946 the Okinawa Advisory Council became the Okinawa Civil

Government at the same time as the establishment of the Okinawa Legislature. Koshin Shikiya was appointed the first governor.

Gunto Governments

The Okinawa Civil Government was composed of four districts; Amami, Okinawa, Miyako, and Yaeyama. In 1950 these were reorganized and called Gunto Governments, and governors and legislature members from each area were chosen by elections. The will of the people was not reflected into the policy areas of the military government.

Senka (Fruits of War)

In Okinawa under U.S. military rule, provisions were given by America but the people still suffered under chronic food shortages. For that reason there were many who stole stores from the depots of the U.S. military which they named the "Fruits of War."

B Yen Currency

The yen currency in circulation before the war was exchanged for equivalent B Yen currency issued by the U.S. Military Government. For a short time after the war this currency was used simultaneously with the new yen issued by the Japanese. From 1948 to 1958 the introduction and circulation of the new Japanese yen was prohibited and the B-yen was the only legal currency in use in Okinawa.

Mitsu Boueki (Smuggling)

Smuggling flourished under U.S. military occupation. Metal debris left over from the Battle of Okinawa such as used artillery shells was shipped to Taiwan or Hong Kong to be exchanged for everyday commodities. American medical supplies were transported to mainland Japan and exchanged for pots, pans, and tableware. Particularly in areas such as the Miyako and Yaeyama regions, where the aid from the American military was late in arriving,, the practice of smuggling is said to have flourished. Textbooks, notepads, and even copies of the Peace Constitution entered Okinawa in this way. Doing this to survive showed the wisdom of the people and their initiative.

Kankara Sanshin (Okinawan samisen made from tin cans)

Having lost all in the war and surrounded by the anxiety of postwar life, the people of Okinawa placed their spirit in singing and playing the Sanshin. Since there were no satisfactory instruments around, the empty cans from the provisions handed out, sticks, and the string from parachutes were assembled into instruments like the Karakan Sanshin.

Sheets Policies

Maj. Gen. Joseph R. Sheets oversaw preparation and construction of the military facilities and bases on Okinawa. His policies also included the authorization of land rights, the discharge of unneeded land used by the military, the promotion of building private sector enterprises, establishment of bus services, and improvements in educational facilities. Maj. Gen. Sheets promoted the realization of postwar reconstruction in Okinawa. His tour of duty in Okinawa also resulted in the establishment of the University of the Ryukyus. He aggressively tackled the comprehensive organizational reforms, established the Ryukyu Military Headquarters, which ruled each of the Gunto district military governments, and reshuffled the military service members that were embroiled in the resistance of the residents of Okinawa. He reduced the power of the Gunto district military governments that had become a hindrance to the self-autonomy of the Okinawans.

However, despite being termed the " Good Governor Sheets," he laid the groundwork of his policies on the construction of the military bases and a permanent U.S. military presence and rule in Okinawa.

United States Civil Administration of the Ryukyu Islands
The U.S. government believed that a central government was needed to rule over the four Gunto district governments and so changed control of the ruling organization in Okinawa from the military government to the United States Civil Administration of the Ryukyu Islands (USCAR). The U.S. Civil Administration's business was handled by the officer in command of the Ryukyu Military Headquarters, who worked as Deputy Governor of the U.S. Civil Administration.

The Reversion of Amami Shoto Islands

The Amami Island Group was also separated from Japan after the end of WWII and came under U.S. military rule. The residents on the Amami Islands developed their own movement for reversion. Over 99.8% of the people signed petitions for reversion and they received over three hundred thousand signatures from mainland residents. They opened large protest rallies, and appealed to the United Nations and the U.S. president in a broad international effort for reversion. On December 25, 1953 Amami was returned to the mainland of Japan after eight years of U.S. government rule.

The Government of the Ryukyus Islands

Established under the will of the U.S. Civil Administration, the Government of the Ryukyus was a self-governing body with legislative, judicial and administrative rights. In terms of political power it was provisioned to exercise full power over the Ryukyus but, in actuality, it had to act in accordance with the U.S. Civil Administration and Ryukyu Military Headquarters.

Compulsory Land Expropriation

In order for the U.S. Civil Administration to conclude leases for the vast land it was using as bases, it promulgated its "right to lease" in November 1952. But the rental rates for the land were extremely low, about the cost of a bottle of cola for 29.7 square meters (9 tsubo) and the term of lease was twenty years. Many landowners did not respond. The lack of response prompted the U.S. Civil Administration to issue land expropriation laws in 1953, enabling it to unilaterally acquire land without the need for signed leases. It was an unreasonable and extraordinary measure to seize land from the residents.

Bayonets and Bulldozers

This term came into use to express the methods the U.S. military used to forcibly expropriate land. They expelled those who resisted eviction at bayonet point and, without allowing them to move out their goods, destroyed their houses with bulldozers.

Tokuju (Special Procurement)

This term usually meant a request for goods or services, excepting trade, made by the U.S. military. It helped the recovery of the sluggish domestic economy and allowed the Japanese economy to develop greatly. The building of the military bases was contracted out mainly to mainland Japanese construction companies as well as those from America, Hong Kong, Taiwan, and Okinawa. In the case of the Japanese construction companies the government aggressively financed them and they occupied greater than half of those doing the construction and reaped great profits.

The Four Principles of Land Protection

After receiving the U.S. Civil Administration's announcement of lump sum payments for land use, the Legislature unanimously passed a resolution concerning "Petitions Relating to the Processing of Military Land." The details of the resolution came to known as "The Four Principles of Land Protection" and are as follows: 1. No lump sum payments, 2. Payment of appropriate compensation, 3. Payment for damages incurred from the U.S. military, and 4. Opposition to new land expropriation.

The Price Recommendations

In response to the submission of petitions from the delegation from Okinawa, a U.S. House of Representatives Armed Services committee dispatched Senator Melvin Price and a survey group to Okinawa. After only three days of observation the group returned home and issued a report stating the importance of the Okinawan military bases to the U.S. military in the Far East. For the Okinawans the report did not recognize the movement for self-rule, allowed the possibility of the bases for long-term use, and placed no limitations on the storage of nuclear weapons and the use of land by a foreign government. The recommendations were a shock to the hopes of the people because the report supported lump sum payments and new land expropriation to secure absolute ownership rights for U.S. military bases.

Off Limits

Off Limits decrees issued by the U.S. military prohibited U.S. servicemen, personnel and their families from going into civilian areas of Okinawa. They were decreed as a way to avoid trouble because of the protests and demonstrations staged by the Okinawans. However, it carried grave economic repercussions on a region with an economy that was dependent on the U.S. bases. The issuance of an Off Limits order was a cause of anxiety, particularly in the central region of mainland Okinawa with its concentration of bases.

The crash of a U.S. military jet on Miyamori Elementary School

On June 30, 1959 tragedy occurred when a U.S. military jet aircraft crashed on the Miyamori Elementary School in Ishikawa City, killing seventeen people including eleven children, seriously injuring 121 persons and setting fire to 25 homes. The pilot ejected before the crash and was unharmed. The U.S. military declared it to be an unavoidable accident and promised adequate compensation but final settlement took close to three years.

Vietnam War

Before the war Vietnam was a colony of France but Japan occupied it for fifteen years during the war. Afterwards, the country was divided between the Socialist Republic of Vietnam (North Vietnam) and Vietnam (South Vietnam). France, America, Great Britain and others actively intervened in support of the south. Kadena military base in Okinawa became an important station for the sorties, logistics, and dispatch of troops to the battlefields.

The Myth of Autonomy

High Commissioner Lt. General Paul W. Caraway exercised absolute power and caused a whirlwind with his comments such as "Currently autonomy is a myth - it doesn't exist. And until the people of the Ryukyus decide that they once again wish to be a sovereign nation, there will be no autonomy in the future either."

The Fukkikyo (Reversion Council)

The Okinawa Reversion to the Fatherland Council (shortened to Fukkikyo in Japanese) conducted reversion activities every year on the day of separation from Japan, April 28, 1952. To the council it was "Humiliation Day" and they held protest activities on this date after that.

Transfer of Jurisdiction Protest

In 1966, under the order of High Commissioner Albert Watson, jurisdiction in two lawsuits, "The Mackerel Case" and the "Tomori Election Case," both involving orders issued by the U.S. Civil Administration, were transferred from the Ryukyu Court of Appeals to the U.S. Civil Administration Courts. The Ryukyuan Court responded to the order for transfer, but due to the increasing demands for autonomy from the Okinawan residents, the Legislature adopted a resolution calling for the order for transfer of jurisdiction to be rescinded. High Commissioner Watson paid no heed to the resolution and was in command at the judgement. The court decision by the Ryukyuan Court recognized the decision of the U.S. Civil Administration Court decision and victory in the election was awarded to Tomori. Later the High Commissioner was changed.

Twin Education Bill Protest

The "Twin Education Bills" refer to two bills, the "Regional Education District Public Employee Law" and the "Special Law for Public Employees in Education." They clarified the legal position of regional public employees and guaranteed their positions. Parts of the bills concerning teachers implemented evaluations, restricted political activities and prohibited the participation in strikes. The teacher's unions, joined by other groups, saw this as an attempt to destroy the reversion movement and opposed the law.

The Koza Riot

Past 11:00 o'clock on the evening of December 19, 1970 a U.S. soldier driving across an intersection hit an Okinawan. The residents of the area protested because they believed the case was being handled by the Military Police unfairly. Warning shots fired by the MPs to discourage the crowd resulted in an explosion of anti-American sentiment. The angry crowd overturned vehicles of Americans and set them on fire. Police and soldiers in full battle gear were called out to quell the disturbance, but it lasted six hours and resulted in the burning of seventy-three U.S. vehicles. Some in the crowd entered areas attached to Kadena Military Base and burnt three buildings down including an office and a U. S. elementary school.

Toxic Gas Transport

On July 8,1969 there was an accidental leakage of toxic gas from a munitions storage facility in the Chibana section of central Okinawa Island. Twenty-four U.S. servicemen were hospitalized with sickness from it and the event was kept secret. Personnel in the area related to the military, unhappy with the incident, revealed the accident to the media. In response to questions about the incident made by Chief

Executive Yara, High Commissioner Lampert stated that the injuries were of an extremely minor nature.

A few days later the U.S. State Department confirmed that deadly gasses such as Sarin and Mustard gas were being stored in Okinawa, which caused reaction both domestically and internationally. Protest for the removal of the gas from Okinawa resulted in it being transferred to U.S. Territory on Johnston Island.

In January of 1971 the U.S. military began transport of the gas to Tengan Pier. During that period of time, 5,000 residents along the passage took refuge.

The CTS Facilities

The CTS oil storage facility was brought to Okinawa in hopes of promoting industry and expanding employment. The effects on employment were slight and the accidental discharge of crude oil caused environmental pollution. Massive protests criticized its construction.

Junji Nishime

The conservative administration of Governor Nishime lasted from 1978 to 1990. The characteristics of his administration were a retreat from U.S. military base policies and an emphasis on regional development and international exchange. The Nishime administration's policies resulted in the gradual economic growth for Okinawa Prefecture, but were heavily dependent on public financing and the industrial structure inclined, in the extreme, toward tertiary industries without developing a self-sustaining economy capable of vitalizing the region.

The Cornerstone of Peace

As a memorial project for the 50th anniversary of the ending of the Battle of Okinawa, the Cornerstone of Peace was erected in the Peace Memorial Park in Itoman City. The memorial walls are inscribed with the names of all combatants and civilians, without regard to nationality, that died in the Battle of Okinawa.

Sexual Assault Incident on a Young Okinawan Girl

In September of 1995 a rape incident involving a sexual assault on a young girl by three U.S. military personnel occurred. When requested to turn over the suspects to the prefectural police, the U.S. military refused immediate turnover of the suspects based on the Status of Forces Agreement between Japan the United States. The Ministry of Foreign Affairs also indicated reluctance and there were demands from Okinawa Prefecture and the Okinawa Prefectural Legislature for a re-evaluation of the Status of Forces Agreement, but both the Japanese government and the Foreign Ministry declined. This ignited long unresolved problems surrounding the U.S. bases on Okinawa and led to the massive protest rally in 1995.

Proxy Signature Judgment

When the leases of landowners of property on U.S. bases expired, some refused to renew the lease agreements as an anti-war protest. When this happens, the mayor of the municipality or governor can sign the lease as proxy. However Governor Ota refused to sign the leases as proxy and the Prime Minister filed a lawsuit to enforce execution of the proxy order by the governor. The case was tried in the Supreme Court with the prefectural side losing the appeal of the case.

Prefectural Citizen's Referendum

Japan's first citizen's referendum was held on the issue of "Consolidation and Reduction of the U.S. military bases on Okinawa and a revision of the Status of Forces Agreement." The voting rate did not exceed the expected 60% of the voting public but an overwhelming majority supported the calls for reducing the bases and revision of the SOFA agreement.

SACO (The Japan-U.S. Special Action Committee on Okinawa)

This is a special committee set up concerning facilities and districts in Okinawa in order to discuss base cutbacks and consolidation. It was established in November of 1995 with a one-year mandate from the Japan-U.S. Security Commission.

Okinawa Prefectural Citizen's General Protest

This was a large general protest rally held on October 21, 1995 to denounce the sexual assault of a young girl by U.S. military personnel and to demand revision of the Status of Forces Agreement. It is said over 85,000 prefectural citizens participated and was the largest protest rally in post reversion Okinawa.

Okinawa of Other History

WW II: Battle of Okinawa:

The Bloodiest Battle of the Pacific War

Private First Class Eugene B. Sledge of the 1st Marine Division had been fighting in 1945 on the miserable island of Okinawa for six weeks. Continuous rain transformed the terrain into a sea of mud that clutched soldiers' boots and stalled large vehicles, while Japanese mortar and artillery shells poured down in a violent fury that mangled bodies and twisted weapons.

The island, according to Sledge, was 'the most ghastly corner of hell I had ever witnessed….Every crater was half full of water, and many of them held a Marine corpse. The bodies lay pathetically just as they had been killed, half submerged in muck and water, rusting weapons still in hand. Swarms of big flies hovered about them.' Wherever he looked, Sledge saw 'maggots and decay. Men struggled and fought and bled in an environment so degrading I believed we had been flung into hell's own cesspool.'

For almost three months, Army and Marine divisions battled to wrest the island from Japan's tenacious grasp, and when the final shot had been fired, more men had fallen there than at any other Pacific battleground. Army and Marine troops would long retain haunting memories of that island only 360 miles southwest of Japan. It was called Okinawa.

The U.S. military wanted Okinawa for three reasons. American medium bombers could reach the Japanese home islands from Okinawa, its seizure would sever the remaining southwest supply lines to resource-hungry Japan, and Okinawa could be used as a support base for the scheduled November invasion of Japan proper.

A huge assemblage of American forces from both Admiral Chester W. Nimitz's Central Pacific drive and General Douglas MacArthur's Southwest Pacific thrust converged on Okinawa. Army Lt. Gen. Simon Bolivar Buckner commanded more than 180,000 troops from four Army divisions (the 7th, 27th, 77th and 96th) under Maj. Gen. John Hodge and three Marine divisions (the 1st, 2nd and 6th) led by Maj. Gen. Roy S. Geiger.

They would need every man, for more than 100,000 Japanese troops of Lt. Gen. Mitsuru Ushijima's Thirty-Second Army patiently waited in hidden bunkers and on fortified ridges for the Americans to land. Ushijima, who stationed the bulk of his strength in Okinawa's hilly southern region rather than its flat northern area, planned to let the Americans rush ashore uncontested before commencing his defense from an intricate system of two concentric defense lines constructed in and among a favorable series of hills, ridges and draws–the Machinato Line and, behind it, the even more fortified Shuri Line. Tokyo needed time to prepare for the expected American invasion of the home islands, so Ushijima wanted to make his adversary wrench each hill and ridge from his well-armed men.

American troops secured two positions before the actual assault of Okinawa began on L-day, which was designated as Easter Sunday, April 1. Five battalions of the Army's 77th Infantry Division stormed ashore on five islands of the Kerama Retto group on March 26. Within three days, the 1,000 Japanese defenders had been routed, and all eight islands had been secured. Happily for the forces about to hit Okinawa, the invaders also destroyed more than 350 suicide boats, called *renraku tei.* The Japanese had planned to run those boats, measuring 18 feet long and 5 feet wide, alongside American ships and explode them—and hopefully the American vessels—by detonating charges.

One day before L-day, soldiers from the 77th Division seized Keise Shima, a smaller group of islets six miles off Okinawa's southwest coast. Large artillery placed on Keise Shima would add invaluable punch to the coming offensive against General Ushijima's force.

Everyone anticipated a bloodbath on L-day. One briefing officer told Marines, 'This is expected to be the costliest amphibious campaign of the war' and added that they should count on '80 to 85 percent casualties on the beach.' A pre-invasion bombardment would hopefully dampen the Japanese opposition, but assault troops entered the landing craft with ominous feelings. The fact that L-day also happened to be April Fool's Day did not reassure anyone.

Surprisingly, Marines and GIs could have waded ashore in leisurely fashion, since Ushijima bided his time behind the devilish defense lines to the south. While the 2nd Marine Division feinted toward the southeast coast, Marine and Army units headed for beaches on Okinawa's west coast, near the village of Hagushi. Rather than scrapping for each yard, elated troops jumped off their landing craft and quickly moved inland toward key airfields at Yontan and Kadena. Within three hours, Marines from the 6th Division had secured

Yontan, while soldiers of the 7th Infantry Division advanced beyond Kadena–locations which strategists had figured would take three days to seize. By day's end, 75,000 troops had established a beachhead nine miles wide and three miles deep against sporadic opposition at the cost of 28 dead and 104 wounded.

'The carnage that is almost inevitable on an invasion was wonderfully and beautifully not there,' wrote America's beloved war correspondent Ernie Pyle. Troops raced eastward in an attempt to reach the eastern coast and split the island in half. In four days of rapid advance, American forces seized what planners had assumed would take three weeks. 'I've already lived longer than I thought I would,' uttered a relieved infantryman from the 7th Division.

Marines of the 6th Division who headed into Okinawa's northern two-thirds continued to encounter light opposition. By April 13 they had advanced 40 miles and reached the island's northern tip at Hedo Misaki. Only at the Motobu Peninsula along the western coast, where 2,000 well-entrenched Japanese battled the Marines for 12 days, was significant resistance encountered, especially on precipitous Mount Yaetake. In a preview of the ghastly fighting to occur in the south, Marines finally secured Motobu on April 20, at the cost of 213 killed or missing and 757 wounded.

While the Marines hammered their way through Motobu, starting on April 9 Army forces encountered stiff resistance from Ushijima's first defensive positions in southern Okinawa–the Machinato Line. This line–anchored on the Machinato Inlet and a series of fortified ridges, particularly Kakazu Ridge, which blocked movement along the west coast–stretched from one side of Okinawa to the other. The bloody fighting required to neutralize each emplacement made GIs yearn for the relatively peaceful first week on the island.

For the next 2 1/2 months a seemingly endless succession of heavily defended ridges, draws, cliffs and caves stalemated Buckner's drive. A typical ridge had Japanese machine-gun nests on the forward slope and on nearby rises that intersected each trail, while deadly mortar shells from invisible positions on the reverse slope rained on advancing GIs. Artillery, located on higher elevations to the rear, produced a terrifying carnage that swelled the death toll and sent large numbers of shellshocked troops to aid stations with neuropsychiatric conditions.

Buckner threw two divisions against this first line. While the 7th Infantry Division tried to punch through on Okinawa's east side, the 96th Infantry Division assaulted Ushijima's western half. At first, neither met with any success in the face of opposition from ridges that bristled with Japanese.

Typical was the 96th's attack against Kakazu Ridge, a 280-foot elevation that housed 1,200 defenders and controlled movement along Ushijima's western flank. On April 9, Colonel Edwin T. May's 383rd Regiment assaulted the ridge. Hoping to catch the Japanese by surprise, May launched the attack without artillery preparation and sent his men without tank support because of a deep gorge that guarded the approaches to Kakazu. GIs scurried to the ridge's crest in the pre-dawn charge against little opposition, but at daylight a tremendous artillery and mortar barrage smacked into May's units. Japanese troops attacked headlong through their own fire to drive the Americans off the 25-yard-wide crest. Private First Class Edward J. Moskala of Company C miraculously silenced two machine guns by rushing straight at them from 40 yards. As the Japanese closed in, he and a small group served as a rear guard while others pulled back down the slope. Firing his weapon nonstop, Moskala ran forward to drag a wounded comrade to safety. While attempting to retrieve a second soldier, Moskala was hit by Japanese fire and killed. For his stirring actions, in which he killed 25 Japanese while protecting other Americans troops, Moskala was posthumously awarded the Medal of Honor.

In spite of heroic actions like Moskala's, May's units had to withdraw from Kakazu's crest late that afternoon after absorbing horrendous casualties. Only 3 of 89 men in Company L avoided death or injury; the regiment lost 23 killed, 47 missing, and 256 wounded in that single day. The Americans had learned a costly lesson—it was suicidal to launch an attack on frontal slopes when mortars placed on reverse slopes could create such destruction. The only way to get at those damaging mortars, however, was to neutralize the frontal positions. Army units could do little else but attack frontal slopes and hope for the best.

The next day, American artillery combined with naval guns to inundate Kakazu Ridge before the next American attack jumped off. Two regiments of the 96th charged up the ridge with high expectations of holding the crest, but Japanese emerged unhurt from reverse slope positions and laid down a withering blanket of fire that stopped the advance.

All along the Machinato Line, Ushijima's men repelled practically every attempt by the 96th Division in the west and the 7th Division in the east to seize a ridge or hill in that bloody second week of April. On April 14 General Buckner came ashore and told his commanding officers in no uncertain terms that he expected the American line to advance immediately. To speed up the offensive, he brought in the 27th Infantry Division to handle the Machinato Line's western segment, shifted the 96th toward the middle, and retained the 7th along the east coast.

After the most concentrated artillery bombardment of the Pacific War ended–19,000 shells fell on Japanese positions–the three divisions moved out on April 19 but failed to gain much terrain by nightfall. Defenders on Kakazu Ridge mauled the 27th Division and knocked out 22 of its 30 tanks, while other Japanese soldiers halted similar drives by the 96th at the UrasoeMura escarpment and the 7th in hellish 'Rocky Craggs.' The first ray of hope for the Americans emerged the next day, when elements of the 27th crossed the Machinato Inlet and dashed five miles south, in effect flanking the Machinato Line.

The Army's slow progress worried Navy leaders. Admiral Chester Nimitz, commander in chief of the Pacific Fleet, flew to Okinawa to share his branch's concerns with General Buckner about keeping combatant and supply vessels off Okinawa to aid the stalled land drive. Each day on station subjected the ships and crews to kamikaze attacks. Nimitz suggested that an amphibious assault behind enemy lines might break the logjam, but Buckner believed his method of attacking straight at the objective was more practical. Nimitz reluctantly agreed, but reminded his subordinate: 'I'm losing a ship and a half a day. So if this line isn't moving within five days, we'll get someone here to move it so we can all get out from under these stupid air attacks.'

Constant pressure against Japanese positions finally split open the Machinato Line in late April. Elements of the 7th Division seized Kochi Ridge and other key positions. The 27th snared Item pocket, and the 96th cleared the Maeda escarpment. In one attack against the Maeda escarpment, Pfc Desmond Doss earned the Medal of Honor without firing a weapon. A conscientious objector whose beliefs precluded the use of arms, Doss focused on patching up the wounded and comforting the dying. In the midst of heavy fire, Doss crawled from wounded to wounded, dressing their injuries and dragging them to the cliff's edge, where they could be lowered to medics below. Hit by grenade fragments during one night attack, Doss refused to endanger another medic and dressed his own wounds. He continued to help those in need, even when a Japanese tank approached. When another enemy bullet shattered his arm, Doss patched it up and crawled 300 yards through enemy fire and explosions rather than expose anyone else to further danger.

American forces could now move on toward Ushijima's main defense line—the Shuri Line, a veritable bastion of guns, shells, bullets and men that would subject GIs and Marines to a new level of horror. In preparation, Buckner rearranged his front lines. Since the Motobu Peninsula was fairly secure, he brought the 6th Marine Division down from the north to face Ushijima's western flank and replaced the weary 27th Infantry Division with the 1st Marine Division. In the eastern half, the 77th Infantry Division moved in to give the 96th some rest, while the 7th remained on the western flank. In effect, Buckner divided Okinawa into two combat zones—the western half assigned to two Marine units and the eastern half given to two Army divisions.

Ushijima unleashed a surprise assault on the new American lines on May 3. He sent two regiments of engineers around the eastern and western flanks in amphibious assaults aimed at landing behind the American front and distracting the invaders while a third force charged straight at the American line. Disaster plagued the entire Japanese operation. American naval units off the eastern coast spotted the assault barges and demolished the hapless craft, killing most of the engineers. Other barges landed Ushijima's western arm directly against the 1st Marine Division rather than behind it. Marine machine guns and mortars so routed this Japanese force that one Marine released the sole survivor—a carrier pigeon—with the message:

'We are returning your pigeon. Sorry we cannot return your demolition engineers.' The dawn attack by Ushijima's third unit failed miserably when almost 2,000 Japanese infantry, delayed in getting to their jump-off positions, were cut down by American artillery.

The counterattack forced Ushijima to withdraw to the Shuri Line, an eight-mile path stretching from Yonabaru on the east coast, through tortuous ridges near 'Shuri Castle,' and on into the port of Naha on Okinawa's west coast. Buckner began a May 11 offensive against the Shuri Line with his rearranged forces, which must have pleased Nimitz.

Army forces in the east again encountered stiff resistance from Ushijima at a number of ridges, caves and draws. Closer to the east coast, the 96th Infantry Division bogged down for two days at a key elevation called Conical Hill before gaining a foothold on its crest. After withstanding fierce counterattacks for three days, the GIs expanded their perimeter until, by May 21, they had cleared both Conical Hill and nearby Sugar Loaf Hill, which opened a seam in the eastern edge of the Shuri Line.

Along the 96th Division's western flank, the 77th Infantry Division battled through its own hell, particularly at Ishimmi Ridge, a 350-foot rise one-third of a mile in front of Shuri. Before dawn on May 17, Lieutenant Theodore S. Bell led 204 men of the 307th Regiment to its crest, then waited for the enemy barrage that would inevitably come once daylight arrived. The Japanese delivered a deafening response, as mortar and artillery fire mixed with unbelievably thick machine-gun fire from both flanks and the nearby heights at Shuri. By 10 a.m., all but one of the regiment's 60mm mortars had been destroyed, and most of its radios had been knocked out.

All day long the regiment withstood heavy fire as supplies rapidly diminished. By nightfall, the isolated unit pulled back to its command post in a last-ditch stand to hold onto the ridge, hoping that reinforcements would arrive before the Japanese overran their positions. One relief force tried to reach the beleaguered men, but had to turn back before gaining the crest because of stiff Japanese resistance.

Fighting continued the next morning. When soldiers exhausted their supplies of grenades or bullets, they crawled to the bodies of fallen comrades to retrieve whatever ammunition they could find there. Some wounded men asked their buddies to prop them up and put a weapon in their hands so they could help fight, but by late afternoon only six reinforcements—one officer and five men—had been able to battle through the Japanese to reach the perimeter. Later that day a few more men arrived with fresh supplies, but the situation for the 307th looked bleak.

Help finally arrived late on the third day, when men from the 306th Regiment punched a corridor through to the surrounded men. As each fresh soldier checked in, an exhausted GI from the 307th was able to leave his position and stumble down to rear areas for much-needed rest. The regiment paid dearly for Ishimmi Ridge. Of the 204 men who charged up on May 17, only 48 returned on May 20 without serious injury.

Marines fighting along the western half of Buckner's line faced an equally tough task in eliminating the stronghold at Shuri and thus dissolving Ushijima's line. Four locations in particular tested Marine valor—Dakeshi Ridge, Wana Ridge, Wana Draw and, above all, Sugar Loaf. To sweep into Shuri, Marines had to clear both Dakeshi and Wana ridges while under enfilading fire from their flank, then enter the 400-yard mouth of Wana Draw and advance 800 yards along its ever-narrowing path toward Shuri Heights and Shuri Castle, dodging machine-gun bullets and mortar shells from the hundreds of Japanese weapons emplaced on either side. Ushijima's artillery on Shuri Heights could direct horrendous barrages on Marines below.

The 1st Marine Division jumped off toward Dakeshi Ridge on May 11 but gained little ground against an enemy dug in on both slopes. The Marines would move forward a bit, constantly exposed, then be driven back by deadly artillery or machine-gun blasts. Sergeant Neil Van Riper recalled: 'I'd be flat on the ground and notice an ant or a bug and think, 'I wish I was that small.' There was *never* a time when you weren't afraid.' While buddies laid down thick covering fire, a solitary Marine would cautiously crawl toward an enemy machine-gun nest or cave and toss in a satchel charge or grenade. Finally, after three days of arduous combat, Dakeshi Ridge fell.

Wana Ridge and Wana Draw took longer. Marines first entered Wana Draw on May 14 but could not advance against the thick fire emerging from hundreds of positions. One Marine tank crew pumped six phosphorus smoke shells into a single cave entrance, then watched in astonishment as smoke billowed forth from more than 30 other entrances. A Marine could knock out one location only to come under fire from three other hidden nests. The Japanese were so thoroughly dug in that even heavy artillery bombardment failed to shake them. Maj. Gen. Wilburt S. Brown, commander of the 11th Regiment, watched his artillery pulverize ridge tops and thought that 'nothing could possibly be living in that churning mass where the shells were falling and roaring, but when we next advanced, the [Japanese] would still be there, and even madder than they had been before.'

The incessant shelling from both sides, combined with torrential rains that commenced on May 21, transformed Wana Ridge and Wana Draw into stark landscapes denuded of any beauty. Bodies of fallen Marines and dead Japanese infiltrators frequently had to be left where they lay, since retrieving them only further exposed more men to the artillery placed on Shuri Heights. Decaying forms, teeming with fattened maggots, slowly rotted in the muck or were blown to tiny bits by subsequent shells. Sledge recalled, 'It is too preposterous to think that men could actually live and fight for days and nights on end under such terrible conditions and not be driven insane.'

Cold rain caused the soldiers' skin to shrivel and whiten from exposure, while infiltrators ensured that few Marines ever caught more than a moment of rest. Incidences of combat fatigue soared. Sledge, who had survived grisly combat at Peleliu, concluded that Wana Draw 'was the most awful place conceivable for a man to be hurt or to die.'

Ushijima started pulling his troops out of Wana Draw and the Shuri Line near the end of May, which allowed Marines to pour into Shuri. Short on men and supplies, the Japanese commander could no longer hold back the better-equipped foe. And more Marines had swung over to Shuri after securing another of hell's corners–Sugar Loaf.

Upon getting his first look at Sugar Loaf, one Marine described it as a 'pimple of a hill.' Sparsely dotted with trees and shrubs, the rise's 300 yards of frontage rose to only about 75 feet before leveling off into a thin crest. Beneath its serene veneer, however, 2,000 Japanese defenders patiently waited to deliver deadly blows. Combined with Horseshoe Hill to its south and Half Moon Hill to its southeast, Sugar Loaf formed the point of a lethal arrowhead pointing from Shuri directly at approaching Marines.

Company G of the 22nd Regiment's 2nd Battalion, 6th Division, commanded by Captain Owen T. Stebbins, commenced a week-long pattern of rushing to Sugar Loaf's crest, briefly holding on in the face of enormous opposition, then abandoning the slopes. On May 12 Stebbins guided three platoons up Sugar Loaf's slopes, but enemy gunfire quickly pinned down two of the three platoons. Stebbins and Lieutenant Dale W. Bair led 40 men of the third platoon in a charge toward the crest, but within 100 yards, 28 had fallen. After a horrifying ordeal at the summit, the harassed survivors had to pull back. The next day, repeated assaults to gain the top failed. In the afternoon, 44 Marines were stranded on Sugar Loaf's slopes by punishing fire that had already killed or wounded 106 Marines. The battalion's executive officer, Major Henry A. Courtney, Jr., figured he was in one of those situations where he was too weak to defend his position, so he might as well attack.

Courtney barked, 'Men, if we don't take the top of this hill tonight, the [Japanese] will be down here to drive us away in the morning.' He explained that when they reached the summit, he wanted them to toss every grenade they had at the enemy, then dig in. He asked for volunteers. 'When we go up there, some of us are never going to come down again,' Courtney continued. 'You all know what hell it is on the top, but that hill's got to be taken, and we're going to do it. I'm going up to the top of Sugar Loaf Hill. Who's coming along?'

All 44 followed their determined leader, reached the summit, and repelled a banzai attack. Sadly, the mortar and artillery bombardment gradually depleted the small group, who had to withdraw from Sugar Loaf the next morning. Unfortunately, Courtney did not return with them, as a Japanese hand grenade inflicted a mortal gash in his neck. For his stirring words and actions, Courtney was posthumously awarded the Medal of Honor.

May 16 brought the fifth straight day of ebb and flow combat when four separate charges to the crest failed, each one leaving behind more grim reminders of war's toll. Correspondent Elvis Lane stared at the carnage and wrote: 'Corpses litter the gray, muddy landscape. There are numerous severed arms and legs. And an occasional head….Some of the corpses seem to be grinning. The flesh has rotted away from the skull and the teeth are bared. I am afraid that if I stare, one of these grinning dead might ask: 'Don't you belong with us?"

A breakthrough finally occurred on May 17, when a battalion seized a large portion of Half Moon Hill, which meant the Marines could count on increased fire support for another attempt up Sugar Loaf the next day. Since Japanese artillery on Wana Ridge was gradually being reduced by the 1st Division to the east, Marines looked ahead to a speedy conclusion.

Two diversionary attacks on May 18, one against Half Moon and Horseshoe hills and the other toward Sugar Loaf's right end, succeeded in drawing much of the enemy's fire. This allowed a force of tanks and infantry to rush around the hill's left flank, attack Sugar Loaf from the rear, and rout the remaining defenders.

At last, Sugar Loaf fell silent. Seven maddening days of assaults cost the 6th Division 2,662 killed or wounded and another 1,289 to exhaustion or combat fatigue. Correspondent Lane summarized how most who fought at Sugar Loaf must have felt: 'Thank God there are no signs, none whatsoever, that the enemy is again rushing troops forth to try and recapture this hill. I've lost count of how many times Sugar Loaf was seized by us, by them, and how many days we've been here. The silence convinces us that Sugar Loaf really does belong to the [Marines].'

Successful actions all along the Shuri Line forced Ushijima to withdraw south to his last-ditch perimeter near the end of May. Ushijima set up his final command post in a cave near the sea and waited for the end.

Army and Marine assaults in June further weakened Ushijima's hold on Okinawa. Marines cleared the Oroku Peninsula in the west, while Army infantry shattered Ushijima's eastern flank by routing Japanese defenders at Yaeju-dake. Ushijima's men had nowhere to go now—either death or surrender stared them in the face.

On June 18, General Buckner was felled by enemy shellfire while observing the activity of a new unit at a forward post. Major General Roy S. Geiger succeeded Buckner, who became the highest-ranking American killed in action in World War II.

Buckner's counterpart across the lines fared no better. On June 20, 7th Infantry Division troops reached the top of Hill 89, which housed Ushijima's headquarters. When a Japanese prisoner of war shouted a surrender offer into the cave, a huge demolition charge blew shut the cave entrance. Two days later, as American forces entered the cave's upper levels, the Japanese commander stepped onto a small ledge overlooking the sea, knelt down on a white sheet, then thrust a knife into his abdomen a split second before an aide's sword lopped off his head.

Ushijima's chief of staff, Lt. Gen. Isamu Cho, penned a final message moments prior to taking his own life: 'Our strategy, tactics, and techniques were all used to the utmost. We fought valiantly, but it was as nothing before the material strength of the enemy.'

Okinawa became the bloodiest battle of the Pacific War. More than 100,000 Japanese died, a frightening number matched only by the tally of unfortunate Okinawan citizens who perished in the fighting. Army casualties of more than 4,600 dead and 18,000 wounded were almost equaled by 3,200 Marines dead and 13,700 wounded. Even the Navy, which avoided the horrendous ground combat, lost almost 5,000 dead and 4,900 wounded to kamikaze attacks. Ironically, though Okinawa was a victory for the United States, its extremely large toll shocked military strategists. If Okinawa produced such carnage, what might happen when American forces stepped onto Japanese home soil? That dreadful thought hung over every Pacific battler, and lessened opposition among high government and military figures to using the atomic bomb in hopes of ending the war.

A long history of hardship

Okinawa, mainland Japan's subtropical playground, is no paradise to Okinawans. Ryukyu, the archipelago's original name, means "circle of jewels." Lush appearance is one thing, gritty reality another. Life hasn't glittered here for centuries.

It did briefly, circa 1400-1550. This was the Ryukyu Kingdom's "Golden Age," its cultural and commercial peak, when "a highly developed merchant marine conducted a thriving import-export trade with China, Japan, Korea and Southeast Asia." Japan's unification around 1600 after centuries of civil war was Ryukyu's misfortune. A Japanese invasion in 1609 left the kingdom independent in name but a colony in fact. The last king was deposed, and annexation formalized, in 1879.

The "Okinawan Diaspora" began in earnest around 1900, with the development of a modern textile industry in Osaka. Factory work was hell long hours for low pay in foul air amid endemic disease and rampant discrimination and yet still, for many, it seemed better than hard labor in the sugar cane fields at home. Otherwise they wouldn't have migrated in droves. At least "you ate three meals a day," a woman who had been through the mill recalled many years later. "Even orphans," she added tellingly, "could make a living."

Okinawa, for all its beauty, emerges in this study by Brown University orientalist Steve Rabson as a prison to escape from if at all possible. The Darwinian horrors of an Industrial Revolution at full throttle proved more a draw than a deterrent they were miseries to be conquered on the road to a potentially brighter future visible nowhere on the home horizon. To this day some 300,000 Okinawans 23 percent of the prefecture's 1.3 million population live on the mainland, a measure of the economic disparity that persists even in relatively prosperous times. Discriminatory Japanese policies and attitudes are part of Rabson's story, but only part. Small cultures in the shadows of great powers rarely flourish long, and Ryukyu-Okinawa was thrice stifled by China, Japan, and the U.S. in turn before belated postwar repatriation in 1972 secured it the position it occupies today as Japan's most economically disadvantaged prefecture, rancorous host to 30,000 U.S. troops.

What people are prepared to endure for hope of better to come is a central theme of this book, emerging clearly in quoted memoirs and recollections. Eighty percent of the textile factory workers during the first two decades of the 20th century were women and girls, many as young as 13. Labor recruiters made the rounds of Okinawa's towns and villages. Parents driven desperate by poverty signed contracts committing their daughters to years of they hardly knew what the recruiters didn't tell them the whole story of what factory work meant in those days.

"I ended up in hospital. Malnutrition was probably to blame … After that I wanted to quit and go home, but they wouldn't let us leave until our contracts were up." "The company didn't even notify their parents when [the girls] got sick, but just sent their cremated remains back home. …"

"Whenever [the supervisor] talked to me, she yelled out scornfully, 'Hey you, Ryukyu,' or 'Listen here, Ryukyu.'" "They kept us on the night shift [5 p.m. to 5 a.m.] and many of the girls lost weight until they were skin and bone … With 2,000 workers, the Toyo factory was so big it had its own crematorium."

Unbridled sexual abuse and work days that dragged on for 12 hours minimum and often up to 18 hours add up to misery that a more fortunate age can scarcely comprehend. The bright future proved stillborn. World War I brought a fleeting economic boom, but World War II brought the Battle of Okinawa, which cost 120,000 Okinawan lives, most of them civilian. For a Japan staring at defeat, writes Rabson, Okinawa was a "throwaway pawn."

Further betrayal came in 1951, when the San Francisco Peace Treaty restored Japanese sovereignty but left Okinawa under American occupation. Whatever Occupation had meant for Japan, for Okinawa it was no democracy-building exercise it was military overlordship pure and simple. The Americans forcibly seized private farmland over owners' protests and built on it the vast military installations whose presence harasses Okinawans to this day, with no end in sight.

"The Okinawan Diaspora in Japan" is a thorough and sympathetic examination of Okinawa's situation in particular and, more generally, of minority culture in a nation that even now prides itself on racial and cultural homogeneity. It raises, without fully answering no doubt because the author would have gone too far from his subject haunting questions: Why did Okinawa fail to spawn a serious independence movement? Why, down the centuries, were Okinawans more intent on fitting into a Japan whose attitude was patronizing at best and often contemptuous, than on resisting Japanese rule?

And why, after World War II, did Okinawan resistance to U.S. dominion take the form of agitating for a return to Japan rather than for sovereignty?

Okinawa Culture
Culture & lifestyle
Eisa Festival

Eisa dancing is performed on the last day of the three-day Obon celebration to bid farewell to the ancestors' spirits (michi-junee). To most Uchinanchu (Okinawans), this day is a most chim-dondon (exciting) occasion. Young men and women travel around residential streets and business areas dancing eisa, accompanied by drums, folk songs, chants and whistling. Eisa was originally performed so that people could give the spirits a good send-off. Around 30 young men and women dance eisa at any one time, singing, chanting and playing drums to the strains of a sanshin.

Eisa is said to have started with ninbuchaa ("monks" in Okinawan dialect) who chanted nenbutsu (reciting the name of Buddha) and danced at funerals and Buddhist ceremonies when the Jodo Shinshu sect of Buddhism was introduced to the Ryukyu Kingdom. In the late

19th century, young men started dancing eisa to popular minyo (classical Okinawan music) instead of to the sound of nenbutsu. This dance style later formed the basis for the contemporary style of eisa seen today.

After World War II, many eisa lovers got together and started creating their own style. Due to the All-Okinawa Eisa Festival promoted by Koza City (later, Okinawa City) in 1956, youth associations in each area developed their own particular brand of eisa with gorgeous costumes and showy dancing. They also started adding more songs to accompany their dances. They used to compete with youth associations from different areas, but such competitions came to an end in 1977.

People nowadays simply enjoy watching eisa at the All-Okinawa Eisa Festival. Young children watch youths dancing eisa and dream of performing as one of the members of an eisa group some day. Young and old, boys and girls, men and women, most Okinawans love eisa, and they expect to see eisa performances every summer. Because of the current popularity of Okinawa in mainland Japan, there are many eisa fans across the water and even in foreign countries, where eisa is sometimes performed. Eisa is becoming part of an entertainment culture that Okinawans can be proud of.

Many companies observe the last day of Obon as a holiday; on Ukui, the Obon mood pervades the entire island. Around sunset, youths gather at village festival venues or community centers, and michi-junee begins.

Heshikiya eisa is well known for incorporating a traditional dance style dating back more than 100 years.

All-Okinawa Eisa Festival

The All-Okinawa Eisa Festival stands out from among other events of its kind held around the island for its grand scale. Featuring exciting eisa performances by a number of youth groups from all over the island, the festival draws some 200,000 visitors each year. With the Orion Beer Festival held concurrently on the same grounds, the All-Okinawa Eisa Festival is an Okinawan summer festival that can't be missed!

➢ Date: mid-August to early September

➢ Place: Okinawa City Koza Sports Park

➢ Admission: Free *Admission is required for some of the seating areas. Admission to the beer festival is free.

10,000 Eisa Dance Parade

This is the biggest eisa parade in Okinawa, held annually on Kokusai

Street, Naha's main boulevard. On the day of the festival, the street is packed with eisa groups, including youth teams and kids clubs, from across the island showing off their repertoire of both traditional and creative eisa dancing. The parade also features a spectacular eisa procession of 1,000 dancers assembled from the general public for this particular event.

Karate: the martial art of Okinawa

Okinawa is the birthplace of karate. The actual meaning of karate in Japanese is "empty hand." However, the Okinawans first elaborated "te" (hand), their own unique art of self-defense devoid of weapons, which later developed into karate. Created in the former Ryukyu Kingdom and spread from Okinawa to Japan and then to the world, karate today is said to have more than 50 million fans in more than 140 countries. Karate is characterized by the use of fists, toes, elbows and knife-like hands.

It is said that "te" existed before the Chinese styles of kung fu were introduced, flourishing in the 15th century. Cultural exchange with other Asian countries was at its height, and it contributed to the development of karate, with the local art merging with martial arts from other countries, mainly China. At the time when the Satsuma clan (Kagoshima Prefecture) subjugated the Ryukyu Kingdom back in

1609, the Ryukyuans were prohibited from carrying or using weapons; however, they continued karate training in secret. Father and son practiced together in hidden places from midnight to dawn so people would not find out. Between the late 17th and early 18th centuries, "te" and Chinese styles blended together to form a unique martial art: karate.

There are two major types of karate: Shuri-te (today, Shorin-ryu) and Naha-te (which later became Goju-ryu). During the 19th century Shuri-te and Naha-te developed into unique forms with different basic movements and methods of breathing. Shuri-te stems from certain training forms linked to natural movement. Stepping is generally in a straight line. Speed and proper timing are essential in the training for kicking, punching and striking. Also, breathing naturally is a peculiarity of Shuri-te. In Naha-te, the moves look more like those of animals. Also, compared to Shuri-te, the kata of Naha-te are rhythmical with an artificial way of breathing in accordance with each of the movements. Other styles are Matsubayashi-ryu, a merger between Shuri-te and Tomari-te, Uechi-ryu with strong roots in China, Ryuei-ryu and a few other styles.

It is believed that the study of karate was confined to the Ryukyuan samurai class and carried on in the strictest of secrecy. With the end of the Satsuma clan's occupation, Okinawa was officially recognized as part of Japan in 1872. Karate became more popular when it was introduced as a physical education requirement in the public schools in Okinawa in 1901. One of the greatest masters ever, Anko Itosu, worked on introducing karate into the schools and thus made one of the most significant contributions to transforming the feudalistic karate into a modern martial art. Itosu also trained many in karate, including Gichin Funakoshi, who, among others, went to mainland Japan in the 1920s to introduce karate there. This marked the beginning of the spread of this martial art throughout the world. Karate was officially adopted by the Nippon Butoku Kai in 1931, and the name "karate" was officially chosen circa 1936.

Karate survived the holocaust of World War II and emerged to become international in scope. It regenerated and strengthened to take an equal position among international sports such as boxing, wrestling, judo and aikido.

After World War II, the US administration in Japan issued an order prohibiting the practice of judo and kendo, but karate training was permitted. The fact that it could be practiced without any implements helped karate gain in popularity. Later, the development of the karate tournament and "kumite match" was another factor that explains the increase in popularity of karate. The All-Japan Karate-do Championship Tournament was held in Tokyo in 1963, with many teams and individuals competing.

Considered its soul, the kata of karate can be described as a systematically organized series of defensive and offensive techniques performed in a sequence against one or more imaginary opponents and are usually given a symmetrical, linear pattern. It includes all the techniques of karate like punching, blocking, striking, kicking and even throwing. These defensive and offensive techniques are combined in kata. There are more than 40 kata divided into basic and intermediate levels. But all are combined to produce the vital power of karate. An interesting fact is that while Ryukyuan dances and karate are different, they have many common characteristics in the movement of the feet and hands, so much so that some believe karate was hidden in folk dances at one time. Some believe this is the link to self-defense. Okinawans strongly believe that kata are the essence of this martial art of self-defense, wherein lies all its richness, in one word, its treasure.

The other famous side of karate is kumite, or sparring. While kumite is practiced regularly in karate gyms, sport kumite has become quite popular worldwide. In such practice, opponents are required to seek the opportunity to attack from every angle and in every possible way. Ideally, kumite should be practiced as a life-or-death match, but never with the intention of harming the fellow practitioner. Kumite is a unique act of sharing, for your opponent and you are reaching out together toward the total commitment of self and toward the understanding of that commitment.

Along with karate, kobudo, or weaponry, was also developed through the use of various everyday tools. It developed as an art of self-defense when Okinawa was under subjugation and weapons were not permitted. Today, karate and kobudo in Okinawa are considered like the two wheels of a bicycle and thus inseparable. Among the kobudo weapons are the bo (staff), sai (trident), nunchaku (originally a horse bit), eku (oar), tonfa (grinder handle) and many more.

Away from sport-oriented karate, Okinawans are proud of their original karate and kobudo, traditional martial arts that have spread to the world. And with more than 400 dojo on the island of Okinawa, the art is still very much alive and continues to lead the path of the empty hand, karate-do.

International Karate Study Center

Murasaki Mura, located in Yomitan Village, is home to the International Karate Study Center, where visitors can try their empty hand at karate. Beginners' classes are available in both Japanese and English. Classes run for one hour in length with an option for extended sessions possible.

Ultimate longevity meal that you can enjoy nowhere but here

Ever since the publication of "The Okinawa Program," which investigates Okinawan longevity, the island has experienced a steady influx of longevity and anti-aging researchers seeking to better understand the causes of this long life expectancy. After coming to Okinawa they always, without fail, visit the restaurant Emi no Mise in Ogimi Village. Heretofore famed for its large elderly population (even by Okinawan standards), the village is now increasingly known for its Longevity Meal, which is at its core a revival of traditional home cooking. Ingana, kandaba, ichoba, handama vegetables unfamiliar to Japanese mainlanders are locally abundant. Each with its own particular fragrance, hue, sticky texture or bitter taste, these sun-drenched vitamin bombs quickly lose their vitality if not prepared and consumed soon after harvesting. Requiring laborious cooking methods (e.g., removing the scum that rises from the broth), these vegetables are not widely available in supermarkets. Thought to be one possible source of longevity, the village's local crop of shiikwaasaa (flat lemon) and papaya are the subjects of research, and it is noteworthy that Emi no Mise uses this local shiikwaasaa in their acidic dishes. Scientists have been able to show that shiikwaasaa contains nobiletin, which inhibits the development of cancer cells, thus confirming the traditional island wisdom passed down through the generations.

The Longevity Meal with seasonal ingredients carefully

Chef's choice Longevity Meal Makachikumisore with seasonal ingredients. The meal contains 15 different elements, 1,575 yen. (Orders must be placed at least one day in advance.)

A. Sweet potato leaf marinade using shiikwaasaa juice rather than vinegar.

B. Emi-original golden noodles made with shiikwaasaa juice.

C. Rafute (pork belly) simmered in a shiikwaasaa broth.

D. Deep fried chewy treats made from a mix of purple sweet potato and tapioca starch.

E. Jellied chiraga (pig's face skin) starter with carrot and rose-colored seaweed.

F. Silver stripe round herring starter briskly cooked in brine.

G. Pan-fried and simmered bamboo shoots freshly harvested from the north.

H. Traditional rice steamed with chewy millet.

I. Salad of julienned nigana (bitter leaves) and tofu.

J. Squid prepared in a traditional masuni salt and awamori broth, highlighted with turmeric (single dish).

K. Green julienned papaya said to aid digestion, in a champuru (stir-fry).

L. Shrimp tempura with ichoba (fennel).

M. Healthy shiikwaasaa peel rice cake dessert the recipe has been perfected through years of research and is only available at Emi no Mise.

N. Miso soup with iron-rich handama (slippery green and purple leaves).

Haarii dragon boat races

Okinawa's sea-god festival

Haarii (dragon boat races) are festivals held to pray for a safe voyage and a good catch and to thank the sea for its blessings. Fishermen compete against each other during haarii in sabani (small dragon-shaped fishing boats). Haarii, which have been held by fishermen in Itoman City and Naha City for hundreds of years, are traditional events celebrated by people who live with the sea. Viewing the haarii of today is like watching the fishermen of old who used to cross the seas of Asia in their small craft.

While most haarii, from Itoman to the northern part of the main island as well as on Amami, Miyako and Yaeyama, are held on May 4 of the lunar calendar (between late May and early June), only the Naha Haarii is scheduled earlier, May 3-5, during a succession of national holidays called Golden Week. For the race 11 or 12 crewmembers, including oarsmen, a helmsman and a drummer, maneuver sabani boats. Although sabani may not look very resistant, between the mid-Meiji period and World War II fishermen from Itoman used to travel in sabani across a vast area from the Pacific Ocean to the Indian Ocean in search of a good catch.

Haarii are impressive and exciting because the spirit of the ancient Okinawans, who once maneuvered sabani with their skill and bravery and crossed the mighty ocean, can be felt once again.

Naha Haarii

Known as the biggest haarii in Okinawa, the Naha Haarii is the main feature of Japan's Golden Week. Haarii races are held on the first and the third day of the festival. Visitors have the opportunity to take a ride on a dragon boat on the second day, when no races are staged (application at the site), while the ugan haarii and the hon haarii are scheduled for the third day. Music concerts, folk performances and fireworks will entertain visitors for three whole days. This event hosts over 200,000 spectators every year including a large number of tourists from mainland Japan and overseas.

➢ Date: May 3-5

➢ Place: Naha Wharf

➢ Admission: Free

Itoman Haarii

This haarii takes place every year on fourth day of the fifth month of the lunar calendar in Itoman City, where fishing is a major industry. Boasting a 500-year history, the Itoman Haaree (haarii) is characterized by the enthusiastic cheers from crowds of spectators that reflect the strong local color of Uminchu.

➢ Date: Fourth day of the fifth month of the lunar calendar (early to mid-June) *Date changes from year to year.

➢ Place: Itoman Fishing Port

➢ Admission: Free

Itoman Haarii

This haarii takes place every year on fourth day of the fifth month of the lunar calendar in Itoman City, where fishing is a major industry. Boasting a 500-year history, the Itoman Haaree (haarii) is characterized by the enthusiastic cheers from crowds of spectators that reflect the strong local color of Uminchu.

➤ Date: Fourth day of the fifth month of the lunar calendar (early to mid-June) *Date changes from year to year.

➤ Place: Itoman Fishing Port

➤ Admission: Free

The art of Okinawan dance

History of Ryukyuan dance and kumi-odori

While Noh, a traditional Japanese theatrical form, is well known as Japanese-style opera, Okinawa also possesses a type of classical drama, Ryukyuan dance, which features dance, music and dialogue and is often compared to Western opera. Advantageously positioned amongst China, Southeast Asia and Japan, the Ryukyu Kingdom flourished in its day. Absorbing the best elements of those cultures it encountered, Ryukyu itself gave birth to a rich culture based on its own sensibilities and aesthetics. The symbol of said culture is undoubtedly traditional performing arts particularly Ryukyuan dance. Okinawan dance is divided into four styles: court dancing known as Koten-buyo (classical dance); Zo-udui (mixed dance), which appeared in the latter half of the 18th century depicting the experiences of the common people; Sosaku-buyo (created dance), choreographed by modern dancers; and Minzoku-buyo (folk dance), locally passed from one generation to the next.

Another performing art with a long history, kumi-odori (ensemble dance), is the theatrical expression and arrangement of short songs handed down from generation to generation. Content is roughly split into two categories that of mundane topics such as romance, familial love, coming of age, etc., and that of violent revenge killing. With the slow, measured rhythms of Noh and Kabuki, a fluid beauty of movement and costuming, performances loaded with silent expression of emotion through contrasting mild and intense displays, this Okinawan-style opera is regarded as an intangible cultural property of Japan.

'Amawari'

This is the tale of Amawari, a heroic adventurer and the lord of Katsuren Castle, who overcomes the socio-political upheaval of the unification of the Ryukyu period with the vigor and intensity of a typhoon. The two sons of Gosamaru, lord of Nakagusuku Castle, play the villains as they try to kill Amawari to avenge their father.

Yotsutake

Yotsutake is the most important classical dance in Okinawa. A woman dancing in a bingata kimono and a large red lotus hat is exactly what most Okinawans imagine when they think of Ryukyu dance. An integral part of classical women's dances, an extravagance of color and intricate designs serve as a symbol of Ryukyu culture.

Yotsutake and other modern choreographies are relatively easy to see at places such as Shurijo Castle Park and also at local festivals and events, but Kumiodori is seen only at the National Theatre Okinawa, which is expected to become a traditional culture hub for the Asia/Pacific region, or at the Shurijo Castle Mid-Autumn Celebration, held annually in September. Through the music and dances, you will be able to catch a glimpse of the Okinawan soul.

Tug-of-war

Traditional festival for the entire community

Long ago, tugs-of-war were held throughout the island to give thanks for a bountiful harvest and to pray for rain. The tug-of-war was a community ritual in which people of all ages took part, symbolizing Okinawa's spirit of yuimaaru (cooperation). After World War II, pulling the rope in a cooperative effort among villagers was revived as a local festival. The largest and best known of all these events is the Naha Great Tug-of-War, with a more than 500-year history. This giant rope used for the match measures 200 meters in length, weighs 40 tons and was listed in the Guinness World Records as the world's largest rice straw rope used in a tug-of-war for 10 years, from 1995-2005.

The Naha Great Tug-of-War is the highlight of the Naha Festival, which lasts for three days over a long weekend in mid-October. In Okinawa, the months between July and October are the high season for tugs-of-war when a number of such events of varying size take place across Okinawa.

Naha Great Tug-of-War Festival

All of Naha is in a festive mood for the event, with a parade and traditional folk performances taking place on Kokusai Street on the first day, and live stage performances at Onoyama Park and fireworks throughout the weekend. The Naha Great Tug-Of-War, the main event of the festival, is held on Sunday, the second day of the three-day festival.

➢ Date: Second Monday and the weekend preceding the second Monday in October

➢ Place: Onoyama General Athletic Park and Kokusai Street

➢ Admission: Free

Itoman Great Tug-of-War

Itoman City, as known as the city of uminchu (fishermen), hosts a tug-of-war to pray for a good harvest and a bountiful catch. It is held on Route 331, where the East and West teams pull a 180-meter (590 feet) rope. A michi junee (costume) parade takes place before the tug-of-war starts.

- ➢ Date: August 15 of the lunar year (September)

- ➢ Place: Itoman Rotary, Itoman City

- ➢ Admission: Free

A serious bullfight

Bullfighting is a unique cultural feature of Okinawa. It has existed as local entertainment for over 100 years and also survived during the difficult days of World War II. In an Okinawan bullfight two bulls are matched against each other, unlike Spanish bullfights, where a matador faces the bull. Matches are not orchestrated, resulting in a true test of bovine strength and endurance. The popularity of bullfighting started to wane in the '70s, but in recent years it has experienced a revival and has become a popular tourist attraction. A match ranges from a quick one that finishes in a few seconds to a heated battle that stretches out to over half an hour, which causes tournament length to vary from two-and-a-half to four hours. One bull wins the match when his opponent runs away. In fighting, the bulls demonstrate their own special moves to beat the opponent. A well-done technique resulting in victory prompts the audience to enthusiastic roars.

The roots of Okinawan music

Okinawa has long been renowned for its performing arts and is especially famous for its traditional folk songs and music. This is still true today, and these southern islands are the only part of Japan where the people's music still plays a vital role in everyday life. This situation can be traced back to the days of the Ryukyu Kingdom, when the sanshin the three stringed banjo-like instrument found in almost all Okinawan folk music was introduced from China, then modified by the Okinawans and taken up by the nobility. After the abolition of the Ryukyu Kingdom, the sanshin spread to the ordinary people and became the preferred instrument to accompany their songs.

By the 20th century the now familiar sounds of Okinawan traditional songs (minyo) as well as the more modern folk songs known as shimauta began to be recorded, and the first stars of Okinawan music came into being. Among the important early singers was Rinsho Kadekaru, who went on to record hundreds of traditional songs before his death in 1999 at the age of 79. He became so well known that after jukeboxes were introduced to Okinawa his singles could be found there alongside the likes of Elvis Presley. Clubs where singers could perform also began to appear, while many ordinary people continued to play and sing the songs at home and in schools. Nowadays the sound of the sanshin can be heard all over the Ryukyus, and a walk up Naha's Kokusai-dori will likely end in its familiar tones seeping out from shops, cafés and bars, and in more rural areas from people's homes.

Most Okinawan minyo have no known author, but many new shimauta are still being written every year. Okinawan music includes many old work songs, heartrending ballads and lively kachaashii dance tunes as well as more modern experiments which are often the result of overseas influences. The songs also vary greatly from island to island. In addition to Okinawa itself, the outer island groups of Miyako and Yaeyama as well as Amami to the north all have their own distinctive songs and individual sounds.

The music of Miyako is notable for its plaintive, beautiful melodies, and these have been recorded most successfully by Genji Kuniyoshi, who is now in his 80s but still active. Among the most respected singers from the Yaeyama Islands are Tetsuhiro Daiku and Yasukatsu Oshima, who have both recorded many albums. Oshima's most recent

CD was an unusual experiment in recording Okinawan songs together with American jazz pianist Geoffrey Keezer in New York. Of course, there is also eisa music everywhere, which is guaranteed to impress foreign visitors. Eisa is the colorful traditional dancing and drumming that takes place in the streets and accompanies the summer festivals held in Okinawa, beginning in July, when ancestors are said to return.

Among the many hundreds of traditional songs to listen out for are Okinawa's most representative song "Nakuni"; the much-loved children's song "Tinsagu nu Hana"; the playful and popular "Asadoya Yunta"; and the lively "Toshin Doi," which gets everyone on their feet to dance at the end of a party or performance. The song "Tubarama" from Yaeyama even has its own annual contest on Ishigaki Island to discover the best singer of the song. Today one of the most important singers still performing is Sadao China. In the 1990s he became famous in world music circles overseas as the producer and songwriter of the four-woman group Nenes, whose mix of traditional and modern sounds became extremely popular. In 2009 China's own project Shimauta Hyakkei was a six-CD box set in which he sang 101 traditional songs from around the islands. It won a prestigious national record award in Japan and is proof that these songs are still very much alive.

In view of these islands' often tragic history and its position as a former independent kingdom, the people rightly feel that they have a special culture and a vibrant music which is uniquely their own.

Shisa

The traditional Okinawan guardian of the house

A typical sight in Okinawa is that of a shisa sitting on a red tile roof against the bright blue sky. Shisa are placed not only on the roofs and at the front doors of houses, but also at the entrances to villages and buildings throughout the island.

In the late 17th century the village of Kochinda, located in the southern part of the island, was the victim of continuous fires. Since placing shisa at the entrance to the village, there hasn't been a single fire in the village. As shown in this story, shisa, used as a talisman against evil spirits, are an indispensable element in the lives of Okinawans and are highly revered on the island, the religion of which is based on nature worship.

A pair of shisa is very much like the Nioh, the two guardian god statues standing on either side of the gate of some Buddhist temples. The male shisa, with an open mouth, wards off evil spirits, and the one with a closed mouth, a female, keeps good spirits in.

Shisa are one of the most popular gifts and souvenirs from Okinawa. From glazed and unglazed pieces for indoor display to traditional ones made of plaster, various types of shisa are produced on the island. While traditional shisa usually have a stern expression to guard against evil spirits, shisa with humorous faces and in unique poses are also available. Miniature shisa are perfect for souvenirs, and those measuring over 30 centimeters in height are ideal for placing at the front door of a house. Prices widely vary between factory-made shisa and completely handmade pieces. Among the large number of shisa displayed everywhere on Okinawa, there is sure to be one that suits your taste.

Ishiganto stone

Along with shisa, ishiganto are famous Okinawan talismans used to ward off evil spirits. Ishiganto stone monuments and plates are commonly found on the walls outside many houses and buildings as well as at T-junctions and forked roads to guard against evil. It's believed that evil spirits travel in straight lines and that they are smashed to pieces when they hit ishiganto stones.

Okinawan Cuisine

An insight into ishoku dogen: Medicine and daily diet are equally important for a healthy body

Okinawan dietary habits have received a lot of attention lately. Many researchers and otherwise-curious individuals make pilgrimages to the island in hopes of discovering the secret to the famed longevity of its people, and more than a few of them believe that the secret lies in the island's food culture, based on the concept of ishoku dogen.

Overview

Local Okinawan dishes are famous for being unique among the cuisine of the many prefectures of Japan. This is due to the distinctness of Okinawa's food and the use of ingredients harvested on the island as well as Okinawa's history as an independent kingdom prior to the Meiji era.

Okinawan cuisine can be divided into two types: the food served to the royal family, and the home cooking eaten by the rest of the population. Palace cuisine was created for the pleasure of Chinese envoys visiting Ryukyu, while the commoners prepared their meals using Okinawan herbs and ingredients gathered from the island's abundant natural wealth. And it's this home cooking from which today's Okinawan cuisine, known as a key to the people's longevity, is derived.

Including specialty marine products such as mozuku and umibudo seaweed, seafood dishes, premier meats lilke Ishigaki beef and aguu pork, champuru (stir fry) dishes and Okinawa soba, which is considered Okinawan "soul food," a wide variety of tasty delights awaits you in Okinawa. Dishes prepared with goat meat or irabu (smoked sea snake) are also available for culinary adventurers. Since local dishes vary by district, an eating tour of the island is highly recommended.

Ryukyuan macrobiotic diet

"Kusuimun," a word used to describe foods that contribute to wellbeing, is an integral part of the lifestyle of the Okinawans and also the basic idea for the Okinawan-style macrobiotic diet. Proof of this is that the island's tofu, seaweed, mugwort leaves and pork used in home cooking are believed to be the secret of the Okinawans' famed longevity. You can enjoy a healthy macrobiotic meal prepared with locally grown ingredients at various places around the island. In addition, a couple of restaurants offering halal dishes specially prepared for Muslims have recently opened in Okinawa, and there is also an increasing number of vegetarian/vegan restaurants sprouting up around the island.

Champuru dishes

Okinawan culture can be defined in one word: champuru. The actual meaning of champuru is "to mix together." Champuru is also the generic name for Okinawan stir-fried dishes. A champuru is usually named for its main ingredient, e.g., goya champuru and tofu champuru, although it can contain several different elements. Champuru, traditionally cooked with konbu or bonito broth and lightly seasoned with salt, is truly a taste of Okinawan home cooking. Just as people have various ways of thinking, each person has his or her own special champuru recipe.

Champuru culture can also be seen in other food scenes in Okinawa. Canned pork luncheon meat, taco rice, steak and roast chicken, which all reflect the influences of American and/or Latin American cuisines, together make up the fascinating and unique food culture of Okinawa.

Pork culture

'Okinawans use every part of the pig except its squeal'

In Okinawa, just about every part of the pig is used for food except for its squeal. In fact, Okinawan cuisine cannot be discussed without pork, which is an essential ingredient for a number of home cooking dishes. Pork is rich in vitamin B1, which is said to be highly effective in relieving fatigue. In order to get by in hot weather, pork is an indispensable ingredient in the daily lives of Okinawans, whose dietary habits are believed to be associated with their extraordinary longevity.

A wide variety of pork dishes can be found in almost every eatery and izakaya on island, and there are also an increasing number of restaurants specializing in aguu, Okinawa's premium pork that has been attracting much attention in recent years.

As mentioned above, just about every part of the pig is used for food in Okinawa including the face, feet, stomach, tongue and ears. Rafute, slowly braised pork belly in a mixture of brown sugar, soy sauce and awamori until fork-tender; salted pork belly locally known as suchika; thin slices of pig's ear called mimiga; and tebichi, or simmered pig's feet, are some of the most widely enjoyed pork dishes in Okinawa. Mirudaru sliced pork marinated in black sesame paste, sugar and soy sauce, then steamed is one of the dishes that best represent Ryukyuan palace cuisine. In addition, inamudouchi, which is a type of miso soup with pork and vegetables, or belly soup with pork tripe is prepared for special occasions.

It's said to be pork that helps the hardworking Okinawans always feel healthy and full of energy. If you are on a diet, you may think pork is not a good choice. However, it's not very wise to avoid eating pork completely: Vitamin B1, which is contained in pork in abundance, helps boost your metabolism and convert fats in your body to fuel to produce energy. Furthermore, vitamin B1 plays a key role in lowing bad cholesterol.

If you drop by the food market on Heiwa Street in Naha or any of the other markets on island, you'll be able to see for yourself all the parts of the animal that are for sale and available for use in meals. You can even purchase pig face, which is used in soup or as decoration on special occasions, as well as the feet, stomach, tongue and ears.

Typical Okinawan dishes

Okinawan dietary habits have received a lot of attention lately. Many researchers and otherwise-curious individuals make pilgrimages to the island in hopes of discovering the secret to the famed longevity of its people, and more than a few of them believe that the secret lies in the island's food. Although that remains to be proved, it's worthwhile to try it out. The local food reflects the influence of the many Southeast Asian cultures that Okinawa used to have extensive trade ties with during the days of the Ryukyu Kingdom. Subsequent circumstances added Japanese and Western flavors. Following are some of the most common local foods that people on the island eat daily.

Champuru dishes: Okinawan culture can be defined in one word: champuru. The actual meaning of champuru is "to mix together," and champuru culture refers to the fact that Okinawa has mixed together a number of distinct elements that make up the fascinating culture that exists today. As a result, champuru foods can be viewed as the essence of Okinawa. A champuru is usually named for its main ingredient, although it can contain several different elements. Just as people have various ways of thinking, each person has his or her own special champuru recipe.

Goya champuru: Goya champuru is one of the most common of champuru. Translated as "bittermelon" and in season during the summer, goya has a green skin and bitter taste. Served at many restaurants, Goya champuru includes goya, tofu, pork, eggs, salt and soy sauce. Goya gives the champuru an exotic flavor and a healthy quality.

Fu champuru: Stir-fried vegetables with fu (wheat gluten), a very healthy food rich in vegetable protein and often used in Asian food. Champuru means "to mix together," and stir-fried fu champuru is one of Okinawa's main such dishes. Found at local restaurants serving Okinawan food and at local grocery stores.

Tofu champuru: The flavor of Tofu champuru is similar to that of Goya champuru. There are not many differences between the two, although in this case tofu is the main ingredient. It is seasoned with salt and soy sauce.

Papaya champuru: Although a fruit, papaya is often used like a vegetable. When added to champuru, papaya is cut into thin strips, fried and mixed with carrots and other vegetables as well as with tuna or canned pork. It is then seasoned with salt and soy sauce. Resembling a cut-up potato, papaya is said to be good for the health.

Inamuruchi: A dish traditionally served on festive occasions in Okinawa, with its origins in the royal cuisine of the Ryukyu Kingdom. Ina means "wild boar" and muruchi means "pseudo"; inamuruchi is an imitation of a wild boar dish using pork along with shiitake mushrooms and steamed fish paste, all cooked in a sweet soup with white miso paste. Available at most restaurants serving Okinawan food.

Rafute: A traditional Okinawan dish in which chopped pork belly is slowly simmered with soy sauce or miso, brown sugar and awamori. The pork becomes tender and free of extra fat because of the long cooking time.

Okinawan shallots: Compared with their counterparts in the mainland, Okinawan shallots are smaller in size and much stronger in aroma. Normally served with flakes of dried bonito and soy sauce after light pickling with salt. Also good for tempura.

Asa soup: A clear Japanese-style soup with bonito broth and a nutrient-rich sea vegetable called asa, or sea lettuce, and characterized by a refreshing scent reminiscent of the ocean. Dried asa can be purchased at shops selling local specialties as well as at most supermarkets.

Squid ink soup: This rich soup contains white squid broth and miso mixed with squid ink, a common ingredient in Okinawan food. Squid ink soup is normally found at eateries adjacent to fishing ports.

Sukugarasu tofu: The term suku* means "young rabbit fish," and karasu (*same as garasu) is a generic term for salted fish. Its saltiness perfectly complements the simple flavor of Okinawan tofu. Popularly eaten with awamori. *Fishing for suku is a seasonal tradition in Okinawa that takes place around the first days of the sixth and seventh months of the lunar calendar, the only time of year when large schools of suku appear near the coast.

Tofuyo: A delicacy essential to court cuisine, tofuyo has a distinctively rich cheese-like texture. It is made with dried tofu that has been fermented in a mixture of awamori and red koji, a method that originated in China. A popular dish served with awamori.

Fuchiba jushi: Fuchiba is Okinawan dialect for mugwort leaves, and jushi is a rice dish prepared with a choice of ingredients including pork and vegetables. Fuchiba jushi is often served as a side dish to Okinawa soba at local eateries. Mugwort is an herb with a characteristic aroma, known for its property as a natural antidote.

Tebichi no nitsuke: Tebichi boiled with carrots, daikon (Japanese radish), tofu and konbu (seaweed) and seasoned with soy sauce. Tebichi means "pig's feet" in Okinawan dialect. Nitsuke describes a kind of food that is boiled and seasoned with such condiments as soy sauce. Tebichi produces a rich gelatin when boiled and helps keep your skin young.

Ninjin (carrot) shiri shiri: Shredded carrot stir-fried with egg and tuna, seasoned with only salt and pepper. Nutritious and easy to cook because you use the whole carrot. It is very healthy and high in minerals, fiber, vitamins, iron, potassium and calcium.

Yushi dofu, kumi dofu: Very soft tofu with a consistency similar to that of yogurt or pudding. It is made from soy, like regular tofu, but after nigari (from seawater) is added to liquid pressed from soybeans, it doesn't set like hard tofu. Nigari is high in minerals such as magnesium and potassium, is often served by itself and is sometimes cooked in miso soup. It is available at local grocery stores.

Umibudo: A variety of seaweed found in the waters surrounding Okinawa. "Umi" means sea and "budo" means grapes in Japanese.

This seaweed resembles grapes and is eaten after dipping it in vinegar soy sauce and ponzu (citrus vinegar).

Jimami tofu: Peanut butter tofu. It is made from potato starch and liquid squeezed from peanuts. A little chewy and sweet, it's like an Okinawan dessert. You can eat it with grated ginger, wasabi, sweet soy sauce dressing or brown sugar syrup. Also available at local grocery stores.

Nakami soup: A fish stock soup with pork entrails and other ingredients such as pork meat, konyaku and shiitake mushrooms. Pork entrails are cooked by constantly changing boiling water to eliminate the odor. This soup is typical of Okinawan cuisine, in which every part of the pig is utilized.

Cuisine born from a mixed culture

Okinawa was the recipient of rich cultural influences from other Asian nations through a bustling trade during the days of the Ryukyu Kingdom. American culture came into the lives of the people with the US administration of the island that followed World War II. With the added impact of Okinawan immigrants in Hawaii and South America before and after the war, Okinawan culture evolved as a reflection of diverse foreign cultures, often seen as the charm of this island. This aspect of mixed culture is also found in Okinawa's cuisine, appreciated as much by locals as traditional fare.

Taco rice: Taco r ice is an Okinawan dish using taco ingredients that have been put on rice. Despite the origins of the taco and the American fast food chain Taco Bell, Taco rice is believed to have been created in Okinawa and has become an integral part of the island's food culture.

Pork tamago: Canned pork, or SPAM, was introduced from the States to Okinawa after World War II. It is believed that Okinawan immigrants in Hawaii created Pork tamago and then introduced it back to Okinawa. Since then, it has become a mainstay of Okinawan cuisine.

Rotisserie chicken: A large number of Okinawans emigrated to Argentina and Peru about 100 years ago. Many of them eventually returned to Okinawa, bringing with them the food culture of their adopted homes. Rotisserie chicken is one example. Grilled with a lot of garlic, a whole chicken is usually priced at between ¥1,000

Okinawa soba

Okinawa soba is the best loved noodle dish on the island, and every Okinawan has a favorite soba place. Characterized by noodles with a silky smooth texture, Okinawa soba is perfect for a hot summer's day.

Typically Okinawa soba uses thick noodles and is served in a bowl of clear, hot broth, made by simmering dried bonito flakes, pork bones and pork pieces for hours and carefully skimming off the scum. The flavor of the broth varies from restaurant to restaurant. Broth with a bonito flavor is lighter in taste, while pork-flavored broth is rich and creamy. The toppings for Okinawa soba include slices of braised sanmainiku (pork belly), soki (pork ribs) boiled until soft and easily cut with chopsticks, collagen-rich boiled tebichi (pig's feet) and fried vegetables. Prices for a bowl of soba range from 500 to 800 yen. Many restaurants serve homemade soba produced by following a traditional recipe. Unique and new types of soba using local specialty products, such as mugwort leaf and beniimo (purple sweet potato), are also available. Some restaurants serve soba kneaded with quality salt produced in Okinawa. Okinawa soba is definitely a must-try dish for tourists visiting the island, and If you have trouble choosing a place to try Okinawa soba, ask an Okinawan for a recommendation or pick a place heavily frequented by locals.

Soki soba

Soki means "sparerib." Soki soba is served in a tasty soup topped with big chunks of soki. It is one of the most popular kinds of soba in Okinawa.

Tebichi soba

Tebichi are boiled pig's feet. These are simmered for several hours on low heat, which makes them soft, glutinous and easy to eat.

Sanmainiku soba

Sanmainiku is dialect for "three-layered pork." It looks like a chunk of fatty meat, but in fact the fat is full of collagen, which is known to revitalize the skin.

Sushi

Sushi rolls, with ingredients like shrimp and avocado, were conceived in America when eating raw fish was an alien concept but have now won international acclaim. However, why not try genuine Japanese sushi when you're in Japan? Traditional Japanese sushi is a small rice ball flavored with sweetened vinegar and topped with sashimi or thinly sliced seafood. At sushi restaurants you can enjoy standard Japanese fare including fresh sashimi. Dishes of the day are recommended for those who want to enjoy freshly caught seafood of the season.

A sushi chef's apprenticeship requires a long period of time: three years for cooking perfect sushi rice and eight years for making the ultimate in sushi, at a minimum. At traditional restaurants, a sushi set (either one or two pieces) with expensive toppings such as toro (fatty tuna) is priced at several thousand yen. However, after the introduction of casual sushi-go-round restaurants, people can enjoy reasonably priced sushi more often. At izakaya (Japanese-style pubs) or at the supermarket, a sushi meal/box is priced under 1,000 yen. Such inexpensive sushi is made by machine, which does not require the experienced master's skills or knowledge, and the freshness of toppings cannot even be compared. There are many ways to enjoy sushi, including large portions at a fishery port eatery, reasonably priced sets in the deli section of a supermarket and authentic traditional sushi accompanied by sake at a fine Japanese restaurant.

A. Maguro (tuna)

Maguro is probably the most popular of all sushi toppings, not only in Japan but also overseas. Maguro, a red meat fish with a simple flavor, is high in protein and low in fat and calories. It is considered the king of sushi in Japan. Top-quality tuna is called toro. Toro is the belly or back meat of a tuna, and only a small amount of it can be found in any given fish. Preferring warm water, tuna populate the seas around the Okinawan Islands, and a large number of tuna are caught off the main island.

B. Shiromi (white fish)

Shiromi is one of the most popular sushi toppings with its smooth texture. Depending on season, different kinds of white meat fish are used in sushi, such as hirame (flounder), suzuki (sea bass) and tai (sea bream).

C. Sake (salmon)

Sake is not what you might think it is, although the name in English looks like that of Japanese liquor (sake). It has a rich taste and fatty meat.

D. Madai (red sea bream)

Tai (sea bream) is eaten for celebrations in Japan as it is associated with medetai, meaning auspicious in Japanese. Tai is the most common white meat fish used in sushi.

E. Ika (squid)

Fresh ika is white and can be a bit chewy, but it is quite sweet.

F. Uni (sea urchin)

Uni is served as gunkan sushi, a rounded mound of rice wrapped in seaweed (nori) upon which a topping is placed. This is one of the most expensive items on a sushi menu.

G. Ikura (salmon roe)

Ikura is also known as red caviar, and it's an expensive delicacy in Japan. Ikura sushi is served as gunkan sushi.

H. Ebi (prawn)

Ebi is recommended for sushi beginners because it's often served cooked or steamed. Amaebi, which means sweet prawn, is eaten raw. It lives up to its name and also has a pleasing texture.

I. Kohada (gizzard shad)

Silver-skinned fish are often served with vinegar in sushi toppings. Many sushi connoisseurs are big fans of silver-skinned fish, including kohada, sardines and mackerel. To become a sushi expert, you cannot miss out on them.

J. Hotate (scallop)

Fresh hotate has a chewy texture and is quite sweet when served very fresh.

The essence of awamori

Awamori is to Okinawa as soju is to Korea. Awamori is a type of shochu a Japanese liquor made from barley, sweet potatoes or rice and it is an indispensable element of traditional rituals and everyday life in Okinawa.

Okinawan awamori dates back more than 500 years. During the days of the Ryukyu Kingdom, awamori was an important import to the Japanese and Chinese governments.

Awamori is a distilled alcoholic beverage made from rice, mainly indica rice imported from Thailand, and with no food additives. This Okinawan liquor is produced using fermented rice malt made from steamed rice and black koji mold, and it is this black koji mold that gives awamori its distinctive and pleasing aroma.

Awamori that has been aged for three years or more is called kusu. The maturation process gives a more refined and mellow flavor to awamori, and generally, the older the awamori, the higher the price it commands.

Okinawa has 48 awamori distilleries, each of which offers various brands of awamori with different flavors. Most distilleries have a tour that gives you the opportunity to observe the awamori distilling process and also to sample their products.

Enjoy awamori

Awamori prices vary widely, and typically a one sho (1.8 liters) bottle of awamori is sold for 1,500 yen to 2,000 yen in supermarkets and liquor stores, while a small bottle of awamori (720 ml) sells for about

1,500 yen in pubs. People enjoy awamori in many different ways, including with water and soft drinks.

Due to the fact that awamori is sugar free and has no amino acid content, it has a lower calorie level than other similar alcoholic beverages, making it a popular choice for people with high blood sugar.

Awamori is admired by people of all ages and is featured in many all-you-can-drink bars and restaurants. One big benefit of drinking awamori is that it does not cause bad hangovers like many other hard liquors. Once you start enjoying the taste of awamori, you are one step closer to understanding the real Okinawan spirit. The perfect way to have a real awamori experience is to go to a cozy, laid-back restaurant and sip kusu with seasonal dishes. In Okinawa, turmeric is commonly used for hangovers as it helps liver function.

Awamori catching on overseas

Awamori has recently been gaining in popularity abroad following the success of sake and shochu. Zuisen Hakuryu (approximately $20) is sold in the United States, mainly in New York City and along the eastern seaboard. It is a popular brand with a deep sweet flavor and mild aroma created by eight years of aging. Kumejima's Kumesen, which is produced on nature-rich Kumejima, is also a popular name abroad. The producer started to sell it in Europe and Asia four years ago. Will a boom in Okinawan cuisine and awamori follow the one experienced by Japanese cuisine and sake?

The certification of awamori meister indicates a knowledge of alcoholic beverages, in particular awamori. Bartenders with this designation mix a wide variety of awamori cocktails at hotels and bars in Okinawa

Habu-shu

In Okinawa, habu-shu is believed to be an effective restorative. Habu-shu that comes with the habu itself costs 10,000 yen to 100,000 yen, while a bottle without the snake can be purchased for several thousand yen

Donan

Yonaguni Island, one of the Yaeyama Islands, is the westernmost point of Japan. The island is known as the only place in the country where you can purchase drinks containing liquor with an alcoholic content higher than 60 percent. Donan is a pure awamori from the first part of the distillation process with an alcoholic content above 60 percent.

Types of eating establishments

Shokudo

Shokudo are casual restaurants perfect for families looking to get a hearty meal at an affordable price. Shokudo are a very popular choice among local Okinawans for a quick and tasty lunch or dinner. Although most shokudo in Okinawa don't have an English menu, some of the most typical items are Okinawa soba, reasonably priced set meals called teishoku and local specialties such as nitsuke, a simmered dish with pork, vegetables and kombu seaweed. There are a variety of shokudo, including long-established places run by elderly couples, those famous for their generous portions and more. These are simple places you can visit with friends to enjoy tasty Okinawan home cooking for the price of 400-800 yen.

Okinawa soba/ramen shops

In Okinawa there are a countless number of places that are similar to shokudo but which specialize in Okinawa soba, including small Okinawa soba restaurants catering mainly to locals, chain eateries and modern establishments featuring a stylish atmosphere. Every Okinawan has his or her own favorite bowl of Okinawa soba according personal preference.

Ramen is a very popular noodle and soup dish in Japan. Due to Okinawa soba's unparalleled popularity, there used to be only a small number of ramen shops in Okinawa compared to other parts of the country. However, the ramen scene in Okinawa has recently been livened up with a number of ramen chains based in mainland Japan launching new locations on the island. Each ramen shop has its own variation of broth, noodles and toppings; you'll be sure to find the perfect bowl of ramen that suits your taste buds.

Many Okinawa soba/ramen shops operated under a system whereby customers purchase food tickets at a vending machine and hand them to their waiter to place an order.

Izakaya

With alcohol well integrated into the culture of Okinawa, izakaya Japanese-style pubs/restaurants are very popular places among the locals to enjoy an evening of eating and drinking at relatively reasonable prices. Izakaya are usually open from dusk till dawn. Most izakaya have a menu featuring an extensive selection of alcoholic beverages and a wide variety of Okinawan and Japanese dishes, including specialties of the day prepared with fresh seasonal ingredients. Some izakaya offer special promotions, such as happy hour, during which you can enjoy a stein of beer for a few hundred yen or a glass of awamori at half the regular price.

There are many types of izakaya, including some emphasizing value for money and others focused on serving carefully selected awamori and dishes prepared with top-quality ingredients. There are also unique izakaya located in renovated traditional Okinawan houses with a rustic atmosphere, those boasting a sophisticated modern interior and minyo (folk song) izakaya featuring stage performances such eisa, shishi-mai (lion dance) and folk music, as well as places staffed by waiters dressed in traditional Ryukyuan costumes. Many izakaya offer otoshi (appetizers) selected in advance by the restaurant. At izakaya, the bill is totaled by group, and later members split the cost equally. So if you want to get an individual bill, mentioning it in advance is a good idea.

Otoshi: An otoshi is a small appetizer dish priced at around 200-300 yen per person. This is a mandatory service and is usually considered a table charge.

'Location' cafés

In recent years "location" cafés with their scenic view and relaxing atmosphere have become increasingly popular in Okinawa. Including some surrounded by evergreen forests and others facing the azure ocean, there are a variety of location cafés where you can relax and unwind while enjoying a splendid view of Okinawa's natural environment.

Location cafés can be found all over Okinawa, but the coastal areas of central Okinawa Chatan Town and Yomitan and Onna villages in particular are dotted with a great many of them. Miyako and Ishigaki islands also offer a number of cafés with amazing ocean views. The menu varies by place. Some offer Okinawa soba and local specialties, while others feature Western fare, such as pizza and sandwiches as well as homemade sweets. There are also healthy-themed cafés serving lunch meals of dishes prepared using abundant vegetables and mixed grain rice.

"Yama" cafés (literally meaning mountain cafés): Cafés surrounded by a lush landscape, usually located in the mountains or perched atop a hill.

"Umi" cafés (literally meaning ocean cafés): Beachfront cafés and cafés located on hills overlooking the ocean.

Resort hotel restaurants
Most of the restaurants at resort hotels offer lunch and dinner buffets featuring a large variety of dishes from Okinawan, Japanese, Western and Chinese cuisines. Dinner buffets often include expensive dishes, such as sushi and lobster and crab dishes. Prices vary by restaurant, with the cost of a lunch buffet starting from 1,500 yen and that for a dinner buffet ranging between 3,000-5,000 yen. With attentive service and the magical and relaxing atmosphere unique to resort hotels, these are perfect choices for people looking to enjoy a quality dining experience. In addition, most resort hotels boast multiple dining and

drinking options, including specialty restaurants focusing on a particular type of cooking and stylish bars. You can also enjoy dining while taking in a panoramic view of the ocean at some of the restaurants located at oceanfront resorts.

Yakiniku restaurants

Yakiniku, Japanese BBQ, is an extremely popular food in Japan, especially among families, and there are said to be almost as many yakiniku restaurants as sushi restaurants scattered all over the country. At yakiniku restaurants, customers order plates of meat and vegetables from the menu and cook the ingredients on the grill built in their table by themselves. For people who put a high value on food quality, the yakiniku places specializing in gourmet meats, such as Okinawa's premium pork, aguu, and Ishigaki beef, are highly recommended. On the other hand, all-you-can-eat yakiniku restaurants are ideal choices for those looking to sample many different types of meat and a variety of side dishes at wallet-friendly prices. There are some yakiniku restaurants offering all-you-can-eat deals only during lunch hours and an a la carte menu for dinner. Most of these places have a specific time limit. (Standard time limit is two hours.)

Okinawan gourmet meats

Ishigaki beef, aguu pork and more!

While traveling around the island, you'll surely come across dishes using high quality meats produced in Okinawa.

Ishigaki beef a finely marbled and tender type of Okinawan beef and the Okinawan premium pork brand, aguu, are among the most popular gourmet meats Okinawa has to offer. Aguu is both delicious and rich in nutritents and is lower in cholesterol while containing 3.5 times more glutamic acid (a type of amino acid that gives it a rich flavor) and twice as much essential amino acid than regular pork. Although aguu pork is slightly more expensive than other types of pork, nonetheless it's widely enjoyed as teppanyaki, steak and shabu-shabu by both local Okinawans and tourists: Its taste is definitely worth the price.

Okinawa's premium pork

Aguu is produced from a breed that bears traces of the native breed that has inhabited the island since the days of the Ryukyu Kingdom. As the original aguu breed was dwindling in number, a prototype of today's black-haired aguu was produced by crossbreeding the indigenous aguu with Western breeds for easier reproduction, also providing a succulent meat. You can enjoy aguu pork dishes at

Japanese restaurants in resorts and hotels in Okinawa. In addition, there are numerous aguu specialty restaurants throughout the island

Shabu-shabu and pork steak are the most popular ways to enjoy aguu pork. Prepared by submerging thin slices of meat in a pot of boiling broth, shabu-shabu is the best way to savor the rich flavor without unwanted fat or odor.

Ishigaki beef
Blessed with vast, perpetually green fields, abundant sunlight and a warm climate throughout the year, Ishigaki Island is a perfect place for breeding wagyu Japanese cattle that are famed for their excellent meat. The secret for raising healthy wagyu lies in their diet. The cattle graze on grass that contains a large amount of ocean minerals and are given feed rich in natural calcium from coral. Steak and teppanyaki are the best ways to enjoy this supreme beef, as the simple methods of preparation enhance its juiciness and natural sweetness. In addition to Ishigaki beef, Okinawa offers the Ie, Motobu and Miyako beef brands.

Alcoholic beverages in Okinawa
Okinawa has a thriving alcoholic beverage industry and produces not only awamori, the traditional drink of the Ryukyu Kingdom, but also more contemporary forms of alcohol such as microbrewery beers and fruit-flavored wines.

On the brewery scene, Orion draft beer is number one, with both a local and an international following. Awamori, distilled liquor with a history dating back centuries, is still popular today with people of all ages and is the beverage of choice at beach BBQs, a time-honored way to enjoy the summer in Okinawa.

For more adventurous drinkers looking for something new and creative, innovative products such as sugarcane rum and wine made from locally produced fruit are constantly debuting on the market. Here is a rundown of what's popular on the local beverage scene:

Okinawa's premier beer

Local beer maker Orion Breweries, Ltd., was established in 1957, during the time of U.S. administration of Okinawa. It was when imported products represented luxury and anything local was considered second class. Now Orion has grown to become the signature beer brand of the prefecture, consumed on all kinds of occasions, from a quiet drink at home to festive events.

Nanto Brewery, a local brand

Nihede beer (a Weizen beer) is produced by the Nanto Brewery, which is located in popular theme park Okinawa World in southern Okinawa. Interestingly, the name of this beer is taken from the expression "nihei debiru," which means "thank you" in the Okinawan dialect. Its excellent taste was attested to when one variety of this beer took silver in the World Beer Cup in 2006, the first time Okinawa has won a prize in this competition.

There are three types of Nihede beer: Soft (kölsch), Hard (alt) and Black Ale. These beers are starting to appear at local restaurants and can also be purchased at Okinawa World.

Helios Distillery Co., Ltd.

Helios Distillery, Ltd., located in Nago, also produces Weizen-type beer. Goya Dry is an innovative low-malt beer that features a local vegetable, goya, or bitter melon.

Other beers among the Helios lineup include fruit-flavored beer, red ale, pale ale, lager (with yeast) and porter. Visitors can enjoy these freshly brewed beers at the British-style Helios Pub situated on Kokusai Dori.

Okinawan fruit wine

The first pineapple winery in Japan, Nago Pineapple Park, started operations in 1992. Its trademark pineapple wine, Lagrima Del Sol (360 ml, 800 yen/720 ml, 1,500 yen), is also available in a bottle with your photo on it (My Wine 2,000 yen).

Authentic palace cuisine with heartfelt hospitality

During the reign of the Ryukyu monarchs, when the kingdom flourished through trade with surrounding Asian countries, elaborate feasts were hosted nightly for visiting envoys of the respective nations.

With about 300 envoys in Okinawa for three to five months at a time, it is said that the native pig population was decimated. Okinawan rulers, keen to please Chinese envoys coming from a gastronomic culture thousands of years old, ordered extensive culinary research and established the tradition of Ryukyuan palace cuisine. As with the tea ceremony culture of mainland Japan, Okinawa's palace cuisine conveys an attitude of respectful hospitality.

Tundaabun

Hors d'oeuvres-style accompaniment to awamori, served between the second and third dishes of the meal. As trade flourished during the Ryukyu Kingdom period, Chinese envoys of the Ming followed by the Qing dynasty would be welcomed with tundaabun.

Popo (top): Pork stir fried in white miso, wrapped in thin wheat flour skins.

Castella fishcake (top right): Popular local fish gurukun (fusilier fish), made into a paste, blended with eggs, then baked.

Steamed fishcake (top left): Gurukun fish, made into a paste, mixed with extract of mustard leaves, then steamed.

Urachiti shiitake (center): Shiitake mushrooms steamed with fish paste.

Fried fishcake (bottom right): Gurukun fish, made into a paste, mixed with carrot strips and then deep fried.

Meat-stuffed burdock root (bottom left): Burdock root stuffed with pork, carrot and shiitake mushrooms, then simmered in stock.

Konbu roll (bottom): Swordfish wrapped in konbu seaweed and simmered.

Tofu-yo

House-style diced, dried island tofu pickled in red rice malt.

Belly soup

Palace cuisine's archetypical clear soup containing pork tripe

Konbu irichi

Pan fried then simmered thinly sliced konbu seaweed, pork belly and shiitake mushrooms. This dish always appears in celebratory meals

Purple sweet potato fritters

Freshly cooked purple sweet potato is lightly salted, mashed and flattened in the hand, then briskly deep fried.

Minudaru (front)

Thinly sliced pork loin marinated in black sesame paste, sugar and soy sauce, then steamed.

Taimo fritters (back)

Taimo (taro) are steamed and then deep fried.

Rafute

Pork meat simmered in a mixture of soy sauce, awamori and sugar for at least half a day. With the fat cooked off, this typical Okinawan dish is a must-try.

Mimiga

Pig's ear simmered in brine, desalted, then served with cucumber and bean sprouts in a peanut sauce.

Tonfan juushi

Chopped pork and vegetable mixed rice served with a clear soup

Dessert

Brown sugar agar jelly.

Okinawan vegetables

Longevity island: the delicious blessings of Okinawan nature

Cultivated in fields with strong southern island sunlight, Okinawan vegetables tend to grow large in size, and in addition they are considered safer than produce from mainland Japan due to the higher levels of contamination found there stemming from the Fukushima nuclear disaster. Although some have a particularly bitter taste that you may not be familiar with, Okinawan vegetables offer a variety of health benefits, which make them worth eating.

Many years ago, Okinawa's hot, humid climate and natural disasters such as typhoons and droughts resulted in a high mortality rate. Long before the advent of modern pharmaceuticals, Okinawans had introduced kusuimun (meaning medicinal foods in the Okinawan dialect) into their everyday diet by choosing ingredients according to the season and their own physical condition. Even today, the idea of kusuimun is deeply ingrained in people's lives and is believed to be one reason for Okinawan longevity. Considered key elements to longevity, fruits and vegetables grown on the island of Okinawa are increasing in popularity by the day.

Goya (nigauri, bittermelon)

Goya is a vine plant of the cucurbit family that produces a dark green, bumpy gourd commonly eaten in Okinawa. Goya contains a protein similar to bovine insulin. Its skin, which contains twice as much vitamin C as lemon, is bitter. Goya retains its vitamins even after cooking and is used in goya champuru (stir-fry). Its vitamin C serves as an anti-aging agent for the skin, prevents colds and burns body fat. Goya stimulates digestion, which can be helpful for people with sluggish digestion, dyspepsia, constipation and diabetes.

Nabera (hechima, loofah)
Nabera is a cucumber-like gourd that is commonly eaten like goya in Okinawa. Rich in vitamins and minerals, nabera contains loofah saponin, niter, pectin, protein and sugar and is best eaten two weeks after it blossoms. It is often used in stir-fries and soups and is effective as a diuretic as well as in stopping coughing and swelling. In mainland Japan it is used as a body scrub and skin salve for rough or chapped skin, sunburn and chilblains.

Shibui (togan, white gourd)
Originally cultivated in Asia, shibui is a vine plant of the cucumber family, growing as large as 11 pounds. Harvested in summer, shibui is rich in vitamin C. Its simple flavor goes well with soups containing beef, pork and fish. In kampo (Chinese medicine), shibui cools the body and reduces fever. Its seed is used as a diuretic.

Fuchiba (yomogi, mugwort leaf)

Mugwort leaf, widely viewed as an all-round medicine, is called fuchiba in Okinawa. Rich in calcium, potassium and iron, it is effective in lowering body temperature, soothing neuralgic pain, decreasing blood pressure and cleansing the blood. Fuchiba also increases interferon, which helps to prevent cancer. History indicates that people used it as an herb and in herbal medicine, and also as an anthelminthic. Its bitter flavor goes well with jushi (Okinawan risotto) and soba.

Umjanabaa (nigana)

Umjanabaa has a bitter taste but is full of vitamins, calcium and carotene, which are effective in alleviating stomach ailments, colds, heart disease and fever. It grows wild on the coast and cliffs of Okinawa and is often prepared with peanut sauce and mixed with Okinawan tofu after being shredded, helping to ease the hot Okinawan summer.

Papaya

Green, or unripe, papaya is a popular food in Okinawa. Green papaya is high in nutrients and is considered a longevity vegetable. The enzyme papain contained in papaya aids in the digestion of protein and carbohydrates and helps in the burning of body fat. Papaya also contains vitamin C and has an antioxidative effect, helping people with constipation and   metabolic changes along with relieving fatigue. Papaya is beneficial for antibacterial activity, prevention of obesity and dieting.

Taanmu (taimo, taro)

Taanmu is a type of taro grown on Okinawa that is cultivated in paddies. An indispensable ingredient in traditional Okinawan dishes, taanmu is rich in fiber, vitamins A, B and C, potassium, calcium and iron. Prepared in a variety of ways, from steaming to frying, this plant is considered to be a symbol of fertility because many small taanmu are attached to the mother tuberous root. It is an integral part of celebrations such as New Year's Day.

Shima rakkyo (Okinawan shallots)

With a unique spicy flavor and crispy texture, shima rakkyo is the perfect accompaniment and number-one appetizer for awamori. These Okinawan shallots are rubbed slightly with salt and then deep-fried. They are a little smaller than mainland shallots and are effective in killing bacteria and cleansing the blood. The fragrance of shima rakkyo contains a component called allicin, which helps relieve fatigue.

Gettou

A member of the ginger family widely cultivated in subtropical areas, gettou can be seen all over Okinawa. The leaves have a strong, peculiar odor and are effective as a cleansing agent and insect repellent. In addition, it is effective as a cure for stomach ailments, regulating intestinal functions and much more. It includes minerals like polyphenol, dietary fiber, calcium, magnesium and iron. You can use it as aromatherapy to put you to sleep.

Shiikwaasaa (hirami lemon)

Shiikwaasaa is a citrus fruit that grows in northern Okinawa. Highly nutritious with a flavonoid constituent that eases rheumatism and has a growth-inhibiting effect on cancer, the unripe fruit is extremely sour and is used as a condiment. It also contains vitamin C, vitamin B1 and citric acid. It's good for dieting and also helps to contain blood pressure and blood sugar levels.

Farmers markets

There are a number of farmers markets in various areas of Okinawa. These are the best places to buy the freshest fruits, vegetables and cut flowers at reasonable prices. Some farmers markets also offer fresh meat and fish. Okinawa has six farmers markets managed by Japan Agricultural Cooperatives (JA). At weekend markets you can often find free food samples prepared with local products.

Farmers markets

Hours: 9:00-19:00

➢ Farmers market Yanbaru Haisai! Yanbaru Ichiba

- ➤ JA Yomitan Yunta Ichiba

- ➤ Chubu farmers market Champuru Ichiba

- ➤ Ginowan Hagoromo Ichiba

- ➤ Farmers market Itoman Umanchu Ichiba

- ➤ JA Okinawa Shokusai-kan Toyosaki Nanairobatake

Okinawa Diet

Okinawa diet could it help you live to 100

Can you eat your way to a century? I am not referring to test cricketers, I'm talking about the Japanese diet. Or the Sardinian diet. Or the Ikarian diet. Or any one of half a dozen regional, usually traditional, ways of eating that have been credited with keeping an improbable proportion of their populations alive beyond the age of 100.

Last week, the oldest man ever on record, Jiroemon Kimura, from Kyotango near Kyoto, passed away at the age of 116. His death, and the fact that the new record holder, 115-year-old Misao Okawa, is from Osaka, reminded us that the Japanese know a trick or two when it comes to living beyond 100. According to the UN they have the greatest proportion of centenarians in the world and a great deal of that knowhow concerns diet.

I have long taken an interest in how I might eat myself to old age. I visited the southern Japanese Okinawa islands whose population is said to include the largest proportion of centenarians in the country and met with some of them in what is supposedly the village with the oldest demographic in the world, Ogimi, little more than a dirt street lined with small houses, home to more than a dozen centenarians. Old folk tended vegetable patches or sat on porches watching a funeral procession go by. My family and I dined on rice and tofu, bamboo shoots, seaweed, pickles, small cubes of braised pork belly and a little cake at the local "longevity cafe" beneath flowering dragon fruit plants. Butterflies the size of dinner plates fluttered by and my youngest son asked if there was a KFC.

The next day I interviewed American gerontologist, Dr Craig Willcox, who has spent many years investigating Okinawan longevity and co-wrote a book, The Okinawa Program, outlining his findings (recommending that we "Eat as low down the food chain as possible" long before Michael Pollan's similarly veg-centric entreaty).

Willcox summarised the benefits of the local diet: "The Okinawans have a low risk of arteriosclerosis and stomach cancer, a very low risk of hormone-dependent cancers, such as breast and prostate cancer. They eat three servings of fish a week, on average ... plenty of whole grains, vegetables and soy products too, more tofu and more konbu seaweed than anyone else in the world, as well as squid and octopus, which are rich in taurine that could lower cholesterol and blood pressure."

Okinawa's indigenous vegetables were particularly interesting: their purple sweet potatoes are rich in flavonoids, carotenoids, vitamin E and lycopene, and the local bitter cucumbers, or "goya", have been shown to lower blood sugar in diabetics. Like most of us, I am familiar with mainstream dietary advice eat less sugar, salt and saturated fat, cut down on the cronuts and so on but I much prefer the idea of discovering little-known shortcuts to longevity; I'm more of a "silver bullet" kind of guy. With this in mind, over a lunch of traditional goya chanpuru bitter cucumber, stir-fried with tofu, egg and pork in a restaurant that was little more than a tumbledown hut close to his campus, I asked Willcox which elements of the Okinawan diet he had introduced to his life. Turmeric and jasmine tea, he said; both potentially ward off cancer. Needless to say, both now feature in my morning ritual.

Of course, your destiny as a potential centenarian will also be determined by your DNA, upbringing and temperament, as well as how physically active and sociable you are; the climate where you live;

the standard of healthcare available; how relaxed you are about timekeeping; whether you take naps and are religious; wars, and so forth. Being born a girl helps: 85% of the world's centenarians are female. But it is generally accepted that diet determines around 30% of how long we live. Some argue it can add as much as a decade to your life. So, the question then becomes, should we all switch to a diet of tofu, sweet potatoes and squid?

According to Professor John Mather, a director of the Institute for Ageing and Health at Newcastle University, it probably wouldn't do any harm but the prevailing scientific evidence weighs more heavily in favour of the Mediterranean diet. "There is not enough research on people who adopt the Japanese diet in non-Japanese settings," he tells me. "It is true Japan holds the [longevity] record at the moment, but if you go back a little it was Sweden or New Zealand." (The Chinese have referred to Okinawa as the Land of the Immortals for centuries, but this probably does not constitute strong epidemiological evidence.)

Mather, who has worked in nutrition for 40 years, adds that the Nordic diet has made a late surge, with recent research pointing to the benefits of its fish- and, more controversially, dairy-rich diet (the latter is an anomaly in longevity diets: the Japanese eat little dairy, and in the Mediterranean diet it is mostly limited to cheese and yoghurt). But he still prefers to point to the well-documented longevity of the people of the Nuoro province of Sardinia or the Greek island of Ikaria, the latest destination on the fountain-of-youth trail.

Last month this newspaper reported that one in three Ikarians make it past 90. Among the dietary factors cited for their Methuselean tendencies are herbal teas rich in antioxidants (including wild mint, good for digestion, and artemisia for blood circulation), gallons of olive oil, plenty of fresh vegetables and little meat or dairy. The US's longest-lived community, the Seventh Day Adventists of Loma Linda, California, also eat a largely vegetarian diet, and the people of Costa Rica's Nicoya peninsula another of the world's so-called "blue zones", places identified by longevity researchers where people live to a notably riper age apparently eat large quantities of beans.

It is surely no coincidence that Ikaria only got its first supermarket three years ago, while, in contrast to the centenarians, the generation of Okinawans born since the arrival of the US airbase and its accompanying fast-food outlets have demonstrably declining health.

"All of these diets work on similar mechanisms," Mather tells me. "One hypothesis is that the secret about ageing is to avoid accumulating molecular damage, and eating fish, beans, nuts, seeds, legumes, whole grains, and not so much red meat, dairy or sugar may help us to reduce that kind of cellular damage." Sadly, the professor is dismissive of silver bullets: "In the early days we did try to link health with specific foods or nutrients, but now we look more holistically at dietary patterns."

According to some, those dietary patterns also include calorie restriction (CR) simply eating less, even of the good stuff. Ikaria, Okinawa, Sardinia to an extent, and parts of Scandinavia, have all suffered from periods of food shortage and their traditional diets adapted to scarcity. Many now believe that reducing your daily calorific intake from 10% to as much as 40% below the western average can stall chronic diseases and boost immunity. Willcox advocated this approach indeed, the Okinawan dinner time mantra, "hara hachi bu", means "eat until you are 8/10ths full" but Mather is more sceptical. "If you are a mouse, it's good news," he says. "If you are a human there is really no good evidence about dietary restriction." In potentially encouraging news for gluttons, he points out that recent large-scale tests on rhesus monkeys have given conflicting results on CR: those at the US's National Institute on Ageing were healthier but lived no longer on a CR diet, while those at the Wisconsin National Primate Research Center saw a survival rate improvement of 30%. CR societies, meanwhile, point out that keeping monkeys in cages is unlikely to tell us anything about human longevity.

So, what have the Guinness World Records' oldest people eaten? Kimura recommended porridge, miso soup and vegetables. His motto "eat light to live long" certainly chimes with CR thinking. His successor as oldest person in the world, 115-year-old Misao Okawa, reportedly celebrated her new title with her favourite dish of mackerel sushi (an Osakan speciality, heavy on the vinegar). The oldest person ever to have lived, Frenchwoman Jeanne Calment, who died in 1997, aged 122, was a noted chocoholic who doused her dinner in olive oil and drank red wine daily. The man the Russians once claimed as their oldest, sawmill worker Magomed Labazanov, who died last year, aged an undocumented 122, recommended wild garlic. Britain's oldest person, 113-year-old Grace Jones of Bermondsey, is quoted as preferring "good, English food, never anything frozen" and enjoys a glass of sherry with friends from time to time. And Britain's oldest man, 109-year-old Ralph Tarrant smoked until he was 70 and likes a whisky. For the record, his favourite meal is cottage pie.

I knew that there had to be a silver bullet somewhere.

Secrets to Longevity

When I think about growing old I picture assisted-living facilities and never-ending pill bottles. Then, there are health problems like heart disease, arthritis, Alzheimer's, and cancer. It's a scary prospect even for me—and I'm in my twenties!

What if growing old didn't have to be so daunting? What if 100 years old could feel like 60?

It's no secret that Japan has some of the healthiest people in the world. Remember Misao Okawa, from Osaka, who lived to be 117? Just last month, a 100-year-old Japanese woman became the first centenarian to finish a 1500-meter freestyle swim, completing the race in one hour and 16 minutes.

However, when it comes to life expectancy, Okinawa, Japan's southernmost prefecture (district), ranks highest for the number of centenarians in the world. Once known as the " Land of Happy Immortals," the islands of Okinawa (or Ryukyu islands) are a melting pot of Asian cultures, from Mongolian and Malayan to northern Japanese. Following a brief "Golden Age" from 1400 to 1550 when the islands played a central role in maritime trade, Okinawa's history is equally filled with centuries of poverty and devastation.

Today, Okinawa is home to beautiful beaches, crystal blue waters, and some of the healthiest habits in the world. While the first centenarians did not appear in Okinawa until the mid-1960s, there are currently about 40-50 per 100,000 population, of which 90 percent are women. (In the United States there are only half that amount.) Known for low rates of many age-related diseases like cancer, dementia, osteoporosis, and cardiovascular disease, the average Okinawan female lives 86 years and the average Okinawan male lives 78 years. However, like many post-industrial societies, where overeating, inactivity, and obesity are major public health challenges, the new generation of Okinawans must learn to incorporate the traditions of their ancestors if they hope to continue the centenarian legacy.

Here are nine key elements of the Okinawan lifestyle that have allowed the population to age so successfully:

Maintain a Low-Calorie, High-Nutrient Diet

In Okinawa, calorie control is a cultural habit called *hara hachi bu*, which means only eating until 80 percent full. Okinawans take in approximately 1,500 calories per day—that's 40 percent less than the average North American. Their diet is high in antioxidants, flavonoids (plant compounds with antioxidant effects), and calcium (naturally occurring in their food and water), and limited in refined grains, meats, saturated fat, sugar, and full-fat dairy products.

Consume Fresh Fruits and Vegetables

The Okinawan diet is heavily plant-based, filled with homegrown fruits and vegetables. Fruit is typically eaten raw. Sweet potato, seaweed, papaya, watermelon, banana, pineapple, tangerine, shiitake mushroom, gobo (burdock root), and goya (bitter melon) are a few diet staples.

Choose Sweet Potatoes

Once considered a " poor farmers food" (as the upper classes preferred rice), sweet potatoes are now ranked as the most nutritious of all vegetables by the Center for Science in the Public Interest and are abundant in the Okinawan diet.

High in nutrients and fiber, sweet potatoes are rich in vitamin A, C, and E, and are a good source of B vitamins, like thiamine, riboflavin, and B6. (One medium sweet potato will provide over 400 percent of the daily requirements of vitamin A.) The most commonly consumed variety of sweet potato in Okinawa, *Satsuma Imo*, has a low glycemic index score of 55 and thus a low impact on blood sugar levels.

Eat Fish First

The people of Okinawa eat oily fish—like salmon, tuna, or mackerel—two to three times per week, usually caught fresh. This low-fat, high-protein food is filled with omega-3 fatty acids that help maintain a healthy heart and aid in the functioning of the brain and nervous system.

Drink Moderately (and Skip Smoking)

Okinawan centenarians were found to have remarkably clean arteries and low cholesterol when compared to western nations, largely due to their moderate alcohol use and avoidance of smoking. Okinawan meals are usually served with freshly brewed jasmine tea (*sanpin*) and followed by a small amount of locally brewed millet brandy (*awamori*).

Stay Active (Soak up the D)

Okinawan centenarians have been consistently lean throughout their long lives, with an average body mass index ranging from 18 to 22. They are active walkers and gardeners, and they frequently practice dance, martial arts, and tai chi. They also take their meals on tatami mats on the floor, building lower back strength and increasing balance through the constant up and down movement.

Perhaps in part to their natural calcium intake and high levels of vitamin D (from outdoor activity), Okinawans have about 40 percent fewer hip fractures than Americans and lose bone density at a significantly slower rate than the mainland Japanese.

Plant an Herb Garden

Ishoku dogen is a universal concept in Okinawa, meaning "food and medicine from the same source." There are 460 varieties of herbs grown in Okinawa, consumed for medicinal purposes as well as for flavor—the most frequently used are mugwort, ginger, hihatsu (pepper), tumeric, and fennel.

Say Yes to Soy

Okinawans eat around three ounces of soy per day, in the form of tofu or miso. Natural estrogen is frequently occurring in the Okinawan diet, with soy containing plant estrogens (phytoestrogens) called flavonoids. The tofu in Okinawa is low in water content and high in healthy fat and protein, increasing flavor and isoflavone content. Studies support the ability of soy isoflavones to slow bone loss and minimize hot flashes that occur with menopause.

Maintain a Healthy Psyche

Most Okinawans maintain a *moai* (a secure social network) through community centers and close-knit groups and can clearly articulate their _ikiga_i, or "reason for being"; they lead their lives with a definite sense of purpose and a deep understanding of self. Okinawans move at a low-stress, relaxed pace often referred to as " Okinawa Time," which typically means nothing starts on schedule. Their optimistic attitude, adaptability, practice of meditation, and strong spiritual beliefs help them cope with all of life's crises.

Indigenous Okinawan Religion

Animism and Shamanism

Okinawa's indigenous religion is animistic and shamanistic. But it is believed that Okinawan animism and shamanism have been transformed and influenced by Shintoism, Buddhism, and Taoism, religions transmitted to Okinawa from Japan and China. According to Okinawan animism, the world is inhabited by a myriad of spirits ancestral spirits, heart spirit, well spirit, spring spirit, house spirit, tree spirit, rock spirit. These spirits, or kami, are considered sacred and supernatural; and the Okinawan people believe that by placating and pleasing the gods through religious rituals, misfortunes are warded off and blessings incurred. Thus, many religious rituals are performed throughout the year in their behalf; rituals are observed before and after a harvest to give thanks for the year's crop and gratitude are offered to the well and spring gods for the water which sustains life; rites are performed for the mischievous tree and boulder gods that may cause harm; and prayers to the gods for any human concerns, such as good health, a safe journey, and success in an undertaking, are customary. The utaki (sacred grove) and uganju (lit., "honorable praying place"), located in hills and forests, are the most hallowed sites of worship in Okinawan animism.

The kaminchu and yuta are the two principle figures of Okinawan shamanism, which holds that good and evil spirits pervade the world and they can be summoned or heard through mediums. Both roles are assumed by women. In the Okinawan villages, the kaminchu is a priestess in charge of religious rites. As the office of the kaminchu is hereditary, she is selected from a specific family lineage and holds the position, which usually begins in middle age, for life. Originally, the kaminchu was a shaman possessed with supernatural powers, but today shamanism is no longer associated with the kaminchu, her function limited only to the performance of religious rites.

The yuta, or shaman, is an intermediary between the worlds of the spirits and the living. The yuta, with supernatural powers of seeing and hearing, are believed to be able to discern the causes of misfortunes and suggest proper action to be taken. Thus, they are called upon when tragedies strike or when any unusual, ominous events occur. Examples of problems for which they are consulted include ill health, dream analysis, suitability of marriage partner, matters related to the tomb, selection of a house site, economic hardships, and even politics. In Okinawa, where women have traditionally held the predominant role in religion, the yuta and her practices are deeply rooted in the social structure.

Playing a lesser role than the kaminchu and yuta in Okinawan shamanism, the sanjinso is a fortune teller or diviner who determines personal fortunes. Men have exclusively held this profession. Unlike the yuta who possesses supernatural powers, the sanjinso makes his prognosis from the lunar almanac, I Ching, and other books on Chinese occult lore. The sanjinso is consulted when selecting auspicious days for engagements, marriages, funerals, buying and selling houses, moving, and traveling.

Fire God

The fire god, or hinukan, is worshipped at the kitchen hearth in every Okinawan home. The fire god is believed to serve as a messenger carrying requests and announcements from the family to the gods in heaven. In the past, the hearth itself, constructed of three large stones placed in a layer of ashes in a box was placed in back of or beside an oil stove and worshipped. Today, a ceramic censer (kouro) is used to offer prayers to the fire god. Together with the ancestral shrine, the kitchen hearth is an important center of religious activity within the home. But many Okinawan religionists believe that worship of the fire god precedes worship of ancestral spirits. They claim that a house can exist without an ancestral shrine but cannot exist without a hearth and accompanying rites to the fire god. Even today, at important religions functions, prayers are first offered at the hearth, followed by prayers at the ancestral shrine. Rituals to the fire god at the hearth are always conducted by the oldest woman in the house. (This, however, is not thought to be related to the fact that the god is a female.) She offers prayers on the first and fifteenth of each month and on all other ritual occasions. Men of the house do not usually pray at the hearth. When the oldest woman of the house dies, the old censer is disposed and anew one set up with her successor.

Ancestor Worship

Together with Buddhism, ancestor worship was first transmitted to Okinawa in the fourteenth century from China. But it was not until the seventeenth century that ancestor worship became prevalent throughout Okinawa. The basic tenet of ancestor worship claims that ancestral spirits are always nearby, observing the life of their descendents. Thus, proper performance of religious rituals to the ancestral spirits will elicit their benevolence and compassion, while negligence of rituals will incur their wrath, resulting in misfortunes for the descendents.

In ancestor worship, the center of religious activities is the ancestral shrine. The ancestral shrine is an alcove with sliding doors about one meter from the floor located in one of the main rooms of the house. It consists of three shelves: the top shelf holds the memorial tablets, or ihai, with a flower vase on each side; the middle shelf holds a censer and two cups; and the lowest shelf is reserved for offerings of food and gifts. Within the ancestral shrine, the memorial tablets are considered highly sacred for the spirits of the ancestors are believed to reside in the tablets. The names of ancestors and some biographical data are written on the tablets in silver letters. Encased in a small, lacquered cabinet, the memorial tablets are mounted in two rows, the upper row for the men and the lower row for the women. On festivals, such as the midsummer Bon Festival of the Dead, and on other ceremonial days of the year, the ancestral shrine is decorated with flowers, food, and drinks. On these occasions all members of the family gather together, burn incense, and offer prayers to the ancestral spirits.

The oldest woman in the family, the wife or husband's mother, is in charge of all religious activities related to the ancestral shrine. It is her duty to watch the lunar calendar and announce upcoming religious rituals, prepare the ceremonial foods and place them on the ancestral shrine, and on minor religious occasions pray for the welfare of the family.

The family tomb is equally important as the ancestral shrine is a place of worship of ancestral spirits. But unlike the ancestral shrine, which is located within the home and is the focus of continual worship throughout the year, the family tomb is located in remote parts of towns and villages and prayers offered only on special occasions. These special occasions include the Seimei Festival when family members visit the tomb with delicacies and pray to their ancestral spirits; Tanabata, or Star Festival, on July 7 of the lunar calendar; and the New Year's Day of the Dead on January 16 of the lunar calendar.

In conclusion, it might be said that although foreign religious beliefs, such as Buddhism, Shintoism, Taoism, and Christianity, have been introduced to Okinawa through the centuries, Okinawa's indigenous religion remains strong and intact and continues to flourish in society today.

Arts & crafts

Pottery

The technique employed in creating yachimun (pottery in the Okinawan dialect) in the Ryukyus was imported from China around the middle of the 14th century and was later influenced by Japanese and Korean ceramics. Sturdy construction and distinctive hand-created designs are the unique characteristics of Okinawan pottery. Including plates, sake bottles, vases, flowerpots, incense burners, light shades and coffee cups, potters produce quality pieces by employing traditional methods and at the same time promote the development of new techniques. A number of young and innovative potters are actively participating in the art.

There are two major groups of Okinawan pottery, arayachi and joyachi, and both types are equally popular for their distinct color and texture.

Arayachi: Unglazed pottery, which developed from trade with Southeast Asia in the 15th and 16th centuries and was inspired by exposure to that region's method of making liquor storage jars. It was first produced in the Kina area of Yomitan Village and is ideally suited to aging awamori.

Joyachi: Glazed pottery, which was first introduced to Okinawa by Korean potters. Tremendous advances in its development were made by a potter named Tentsu Hirata. Over the years, Joyachi made the transition from serving as items for everyday use to objects of fine art.

Ryukyu glassware

Reflecting Okinawa's cultural landscape, Ryukyu glassware boasts extremely unique designs and vivid colors that remind one of the island's natural beauties. Including tableware for everyday use and smaller items ideal for souvenirs, various kinds of Ryukyu glass products are available. Their formal tableware is perfect for special occasions.

Up until the end of World War II, Okinawan glass production consisted mostly of everyday items. However, after war, large quantities of soft drink bottles discarded by American forces on Okinawa were remade into glasses by local craftsmen. The Americans appreciated the alluring handmade glass, and after the reversion of Okinawa to Japan, Ryukyu glass gained in popularity as souvenirs for tourists and has become a familiar Okinawan craft. Since then, glass-making artisans have created a new style of glassware with their constantly evolving, innovative ideas.

The glassware is being improved through intensive research and development, expansion of its variety of uses and the introduction of new materials to create unique designs and colors. Although it is relatively thick and unevenly formed, Ryukyu glassware is eminently practical, while mainland glass is evenly shaped but not practical for daily use. The vivid colors and unique designs are popular with tourists.

Textiles

Okinawan textiles developed under the influence of fabrics from Southeast Asia, China and mainland Japan. The rich variety and technique of Okinawan textiles are beyond compare, even surpassing those of mainland Japan. Okinawa is blessed with a variety of subtropical plants that can be used to dye textiles. Turmeric produces yellow pigment, and Japanese bayberry results in brown. And several different kinds of plant pigments are mixed to achieve a wide color range.

Bingata, the epitome of dyed Okinawan work, is identified by its beautiful array of radiant colors, including vermilion, purple, indigo, yellow and green. It was used for royal attire and also for clothes worn by court entertainers. Bingata is an important craft representing the Ryukyu culture.

Traditionally grown on Okinawa, Ryukyu indigo is valued for its color, darker than other types of indigo. Although it was once commonly produced throughout the northern Okinawa region, the only production site today is in Motobu. Uujizome, characterized by its distinct green and yellow coloring, is a recently developed form of dyed textile using sugarcane leaf extract and is very popular with tourists and locals alike

Bingata

Bingata is a traditional Okinawan textile in which colorful designs are stenciled onto cotton or linen fabric. In production since the days of the Ryukyu Kingdom, bingata is still being created by artisans in both age-old and more modern designs and media.

Basho-fu

Basho-fu is the oldest of all Okinawan handwoven textiles. Due to a decline in the number of basho (Japanese banana) plants, it has become a valuable textile produced only in Ogimi Village in the north of Okinawa's main island.

Minsa

Of all the minsa in Okinawa, that of Yaeyama is the best known. The alternating pattern of five and four small rectangles symbolizes "love forever," because of which a woman in olden times would give this textile to the man she loved. The handwoven piece was also believed to protect the person who received it.

Ujizome

This textile is handwoven and dyed with sugarcane extract, resulting in distinctly brilliant green and yellow designs. Both tourists and locals have taken a liking to this uniquely colored fabric.

Yomitanzan-hanaori

Yomitanzan-hanaori, originally limited to court circles during the Ryukyu dynasty, is made from silk or cotton and features geometric designs or colorful patterns. Flowers are created on the fabric by means of small dots of fiber.

Traditional Okinawan jewelry

Metal arts inherited from the Ryukyu Kingdom

In the days of the Ryukyu Kingdom Okinawan women used to do their hair up with jiifaa, or traditional silver hairpins. Kenji Matayoshi, a descendant of a family that worked silver for royalty, is an artisan called a kugani-jeeku, one who makes jiifaa of the old days. Kugani-jeeku in the Rykyuan language is transcribed as "goldsmith" in kanji, but kugani (gold) is also a general term for metals, and Matayoshi specializes in silverwork in particular. Although the traditional technique of silverwork had almost disappeared after the upheaval of World War II, the subsequent U.S. occupation of Okinawa and its reversion to Japan, the technique was revived by Matayoshi's predecessor in the 1960s, and silverwork such as the jiifaa, the fusa-ring and the musubi-ring one again came into being. Matayoshi is the heir of such Ryukyuan silverwork. Every day at his workshop in Shuri you can hear the sound of him beating silver with a hammer.

Lacquerware

Produced in Okinawa's unique subtropical environment, Ryukyu lacquerware is characterized by the vividness of its contrasting blacks and reds. Okinawa fortunately possesses the fine native woods ideal for lacquerware including deigo, suitable for serving trays and bowls because it rarely becomes deformed or cracked; sendan (chinaberry tree) with a beautiful grain; and banyan trees. Ryukyu lacquerware is produced using various sophisticated techniques. For example, in products known as chinpin, powdered gold is inlaid in lacquerware, creating beautiful patterns. Although cheap, mass-produced lacquerware is sold at reasonable prices at souvenir shops, artisans still employ the traditional technique of the Ryukyu Kingdom era, making each piece by hand.

Okinawa: An Island with multiple Culture in Her Home

I might not have noticed the three distinct cultures of Okinawa prior to living in Taos I might have simply assumed the Okinawans were Japanese, when in fact they are no more Japanese than Native Americans in Taos with Spanish Christian names are necessarily Hispanic. The three cultures come together in ways that are both reminiscent and dissimilar to Taos.

The Okinawans are descendant from a distinct Asian people called the Ryukyu, which were first recognized by the Chinese in the 6th century. They carry the same ancestry as some Chinese and Taiwanese families, but they are distinct in both appearance and tradition. Some of the earliest Ryukyu people continued on their journeys to the eastern and northernmost islands to settle Japan. Okinawa was captured in the 17th century by Satsuma-han of the Japanese mainland, and was formally integrated into the Japanese kingdom upon the kidnapping of the last Okinawan king in 1871. The two languages the Uchinaguchi of Okinawa and Japanese are related, but distinct. Okinawa is considered subject to, and their language relegated to being deemed a dialect of, Japanese. The Ryukyu descendants have maintained their own religion, which is a blend of Shintoan ancestor worship, Buddhist deity worship and pure animistic shamanism. They have distinct foods that are neither Chinese nor Japanese, but rather some blend of the two. Pork, seafood, soba noodles and Awamori a rice wine similar to but quite distinct from Sake (through the use of herbal tonics within it) are all common. The Okinawans are known for their black evaporated salt as well as their dark-brown sugars made from sugar cane raised on the island. Rice is not grown here, at least not on a mass scale.

It is clearly evident that the Japanese have had a great influence on the Okinawans, through the use of the common language (Okinawan dialect was banned in practice until last century, much like the Native Americans were banned from speaking their native tongues); the most ancient forms of Okinawan homes are very similar to Japanese wooden houses; and the Okinawans borrow cultural traditions like taking shoes off when entering a house or business. Japanese influence is also clearly demonstrated by the Okinawan's reputation of having studious, harmonious and industrious natures. Japanese tourists are plentiful, as they reach into the most ancient of their past to see where they came from.

The Okinawans are quick to let you know they are Japanese only by happenstance, and their rich cultural heritage confirms this. Vast castle ruins of their own feudal lords, a unique style of kimono, and dissimilar dance and music forms clearly illustrate the differences between the Ryukyuan and Japanese cultures. The Okinawans also modified the traditional wooden house forms to use concrete, bars over windows, and glued-on tile roofs to deal with their common typhoons. The architecture that results is industrial, but also decorated, resulting in a marriage of forms that appears both Prairie-style and Art Deco at once. The use of Shisa, or guardian lion-dogs, borders on a requirement and nearly every business and home is decorated with them. The Okinawans also reserve the most sacred spots of land for their plentiful necropoli and there are entire weeks of festivals where the family spends the week at the tomb of their forebears. The Okinawans are known as being very non-Japanese in that they are easy-going, talkative and positive.

After World War II, the United States captured Okinawa and kept part of her for use by 13 Army, Navy, Marine and Air Force bases. In the heavily inhabited central section of the island, where the Americans are ever present with lines of American women pushing endless streams of baby carriages the island is wrought with overcrowding and the stress of a military force that is dominant. Few non-natives attempt to learn the language(s) and others without their own families for years on end act out their frustrations on each other, giving the Americans here the challenging situation of being seen as the "second oppressors." Protests of the bases by the Okinawans are common. Even with these challenges, the Americans that do embrace the Okinawan experience find a rich heritage and a rich people who are more than willing to share it. The American presence very likely has contributed to Karate-do a martial art that resulted from the banning of Okinawans possessing arms so they could not resist the Japanese that was formed of the merging of Kung Fu from China and purely Okinawan movement practices. It has become the most popular martial art practiced in the world. This tiny string of islands, 56 miles long and 26 miles wide, has had a massive emotional impact on all the Americans who have come to call it home, even for a time.

The abundant resources provided by both Japanese and American tourists have helped the Okinawans restore many of their ancient temples and castles that were destroyed in the war. Entire industries have risen to meet the tourism prospects, with four ancient Ryukyu themed parks on the island as well as various orchards and pottery villages that find ways of surviving on tourism dollars.

Somehow in the milieu, there is a peacefulness about this place and her cultures trying to manage the situation of living together. The Okinawan people are kind and gentle. If one even attempts to speak Japanese, and especially if attempting Uchinaguchi itself, the Okinawan will smile and help you say the right words in the right way, then pat you on the arm or back when you get it right, finally. When asking for directions, they will take your hand and walk you to where you want to go. A glimpse into the garden, if you are caught peeking, will result in a tiny little Okinawan rushing out to take your hand and walk you through the hand-crafted garden shrines that Okinawans are proud to create in their gardens.

It's as if each home needs a place for the god(s) to rest, so they create amazing little worlds of mountains, bonsai as big as houses, waterfalls and koi ponds, and beautiful plants and flowers for the gods to be surrounded and entertained with. They are proud of their culture, their religion, their history, and as long as you are respectful, take off your shoes before entering, and are polite, they will try and teach you what they know, even if it's in Japanese. They assume some of the lesson will stick, even if you can't actually understand what they are saying.

On a recent trip to an Okinawan beach which are quite distinct from the vast sprawling sands of the American-favored beaches in that they are rich with foliage, caves and rock outcrops a group of four little Okinawan ladies was walking the hiking trails behind me. I found myself singing a song of offering to the East China Sea from a beach cave and they waited 'til I finished to come in. As I turned around to pass them and leave to do more hiking, I realized they were at an altar at a tiny little cave going down into the earth behind me, making offerings, as it is the women of this island who are the priests and family ministers. I suppose I had made an offering too, in my song. They smiled at me, and I left them to do their work. A little later, further up the path, as I stopped to rest under a beautiful rock outcrop and attempt to write a haiku, they caught up to me and went about their chatting and observations.

One pretended to push a great rock over, as if it were her intent to steal it for her own celestial garden. They proceeded to explain to me in Japanese that I do not understand, supplemented by gestures and my own personal background that allowed me to comprehend what a scholar's rock was for: a place of respite, to mentally project oneself into while meditating, and a place for the gods to reside. Being a bit of a Asiaphile, I knew what the stones are used for within the garden, but it was them reaching out to me for no other reason than sensing I was interested and wanting to participate in their culture that struck me. Tears formed and I bowed repeatedly in gratitude to them once they finished the teaching. I couldn't help but be honored that they decided to share themselves and their traditions with me. And by doing so, they guaranteed a little piece of their culture would carry on. For after all, now I get to share the story with you and it is in you now too.